Diaspora Identities

Susanne Lachenicht is Professor of Early Modern History at Bayreuth University. *Kirsten Heinsohn* is a research fellow at the Institute for German-Jewish History in Hamburg and a lecturer at Hamburg University.

Susanne Lachenicht, Kirsten Heinsohn (eds.)

Diaspora Identities

Exile, Nationalism and Cosmopolitanism in Past and Present

Campus Verlag
Frankfurt/New York

Gedruckt mit Unterstützung der Fritz Thyssen Stiftung für Wissenschaftsförderung

Bibliographic Information published by the Deutsche Nationalbibliothek.
Die Deutsche Nationalbibliothek lists this publication in the Deutsche Nationalbibliografie; detailed bibliographic data are available in the Internet at http://dnb.d-nb.de.
ISBN 978-3-593-38819-9

Cover illustration: © www.photocase.de
Cover design: Campus Verlag

Printing office and bookbinder:
Printed on acid free paper.
Printed in Germany

For further information:
www.campus.de
www.press.uchicago.edu

Table of Contents

Diaspora Identities: Exile, Nationalism and Cosmopolitanism in Past and Present – An introduction

Susanne Lachenicht/Kirsten Heinsohn

At the turn of the 21st century, social sciences started to re-introduce the concept of cosmopolitanism (Vertovec and Cohen 2002; Cheah and Bruce Robbins 1998; Beck and Grande 2004; Beck 2004). Daniele Archibugi argues that the (post)modern notion of cosmopolitanism consists of three interrelated principles: tolerance, democratic legitimacy and effectiveness (Archibugi 2003, 11). Ulrich Beck sees cosmopolitanism as a »specific form of social interaction with cultural distinctness« (Beck 2004, 25). Cosmopolitanism now comes across as a positive concept which relies on values drafted by protagonists of the Enlightenment (Kleingeld and Brown 2002), but which has also been tinged by postcolonial or postmodern studies (Nussbaum 1996; Nussbaum and Cohen 1996). Universal human values such as the equality of religions and ethnicities are supposed to co-exist with local, regional, gender, religious, ethnic and national distinctiveness. Post-modern cosmopolitanism is meant to enable people and societies to tackle problems arising from globalisation and the emergence of new nationalisms. It also provides a new paradigm for academic research on nationalism and diaspora in past and present.

Social scientists and historians have often claimed that postmodernism left academia with a vacuum with regard to politics, values and ethical standards owing to its inherent relativism. The »ethical turn« in social sciences and the humanities (Rosenfeld 2006; Davis and Womack 2001; Lubkoll and Wischmeyer 2009) has given rise to studies on (and claims to rights of) indigenous populations, historical ethical standards, minorities and diasporas (Dickason 1997; Berlin 2003; Bloxham 2005; Thompson 2006; Lutz 2007; Gallois 2009).

Comparative studies on the interrelatedness of exile or diasporas, cosmopolitanism and nationalism are scarce. Most work on nationalism refers to the modern period, which covers, roughly, the nineteenth and twentieth centuries. Looking at notions and the historical meaning of nations, nationhood and nationalism(s) in a late antique, medieval or early modern perspective could reveal more about the contexts in which nations are shaped and nationalisms arise. Hence in a broader perspective, nations can be defined as ethnic, religious or cultural communities which do not necessarily relate themselves to a territory or a nation-state. However, they do perceive themselves (or are perceived) as a distinct group apart. Dealing with different notions and concepts of nation and nationalism, out of which present-day concepts evolved, a comparative approach to nations and nationalism could help to understand patterns of belonging and separation over time and space. It could also enable historians of all periods to gain from each others' expertise.

The formation of distinct barriers between nations was and is meant to protect »imagined communities« (Benedict Anderson) against other communities that seem to be at odds with one's own community or threaten its very existence. In the modern period, more often than not, nations were constructed within a distinct territory. A leading group attempted to achieve sovereignty for their nation and to maintain their distinct culture, language and sometimes one unifying religion, with one myth about the emergence of the nation and with specific institutions forming the state's government. Those are meant to guarantee the distinctiveness and the economic, political and cultural survival of the nation.

However, nation-states are only one option. As Daniel and Jonathan Boyarin (1993) suggest, nations can rise and survive in entirely different settings. If we look at the characteristics of a nation as developed above, these are fundamental to diaspora communities as well – excluding in some ways the territory or the state aspect. However, many of these diasporas make efforts to form a sovereign nation-state such as the Sikh diaspora; others, such as the Jewish or the Irish diasporas, already have homelands indeed.

Exile or diasporas can encourage nationalism: the notion and the dream of the homeland become strong uniting elements (Cohen 1997, 106). Other diasporas, though, or at least some representatives of these diasporas see cosmopolitan elements at the very heart of the nation in question. With regard to the specific history of the Jewish Diaspora, the Boyarins suggest that despite all dangers of antagonizing the host societies in which they find themselves, the Jewish Diaspora tradition must continue to insist on the respect for difference »within a world grown thoroughly and inextricably interdependent« (Boyarin 1993, 723). Jewish identity can never anchor itself in a self-satisfied resting place, or manifest itself as a form of nativism; it has to find expression through a perpetual, creative diasporic tension. In this deterritorialised notion of Jewish identity the Boyarins find a new idea as powerful as the Jews' contribution to the notion of monotheism: »peoples and homelands are not necessarily and originally linked« (Cohen 1997, 127).

Today, globalisation, though not a new phenomenon, is one of the driving forces in the economy, politics and culture of different societies; political and social sciences have opened up to the concept of cosmopolitanism as a means of responding to the challenges of globalisation (Vertovec and Cohen 2002). Cosmopolitanism is referred to as »hybridity«, which has been used »to denote the evolution of new dynamic, mixed cultures«. Robin Cohen prefers »the long established concept of syncretism – the evolution of commingled cultures that are different from two or more parent cultures« (Cohen 1997, 130–131). However, the postmodernist »dissolution of authentically national cultural life into multinational eclecticism« (Shusterman 1993, 302) is not generally accepted. Universal principles, such as human rights, democracy and the acceptance of »otherness« (Beck and Grande 2004, 27), can be at odds with new nationalisms, local, regional and religious identities that seem to evolve as a counterpart to what is perceived as global homogenisation

Our hypothesis is twofold:

I) Cosmopolitanism and nationalism are two antagonistic concepts that are, in situations of exile or diasporas, necessarily complementary.
II) The formation of the nation-states have been influenced and formed by nation-states and trans-national and even supra-national nations or diasporas that were not part of the dominant nation and culture (Lachenicht 2007) as the examples of the Huguenots, Sephardi Jews or other diasporas in various early modern states make evident.

The volume aims to present different perspectives on exile and diasporas and their consequences for groups and identity formation in trans-national contexts. It attempts to define and explain the rise of nationalisms and nation-states in the context of and in confrontation with exiles and diasporas. It will shed new light on historical varieties and definitions of cultural, political or social cosmopolitanism (or cosmopolitan attitudes and practices). Many contributions are concerned with the interconnectedness of or the creative tension between cosmopolitanism and nationalism in exile or diaspora. We also investigate the role of the homeland, religion and the formation of the nation-state in generating national identities.

Liam Chambers argues in *»Une Seconde Patrie«: The Irish Colleges, Paris, in the Eighteenth and Nineteenth Centuries* that the administrators, students and priests of the Irish Colleges in Paris developed a strong sense of Irish Catholic identity. However, they simultaneously fostered »an adaptable approach to identity, which encompassed Irish, British and French aspects« to gain access to economic resources and to guarantee the survival of the Irish colleges abroad. Chambers emphasises that during the nineteenth century it became more difficult to maintain a flexible and thus pragmatic approach to Irish Catholic identity in France, partly as a result of increasing nationalisms.

As early as the sixteenth century, pragmatic approaches to identity formation, hybridity or ambivalence, could raise suspicion, as the example of the Portuguese Jewish Diaspora in the Atlantic World shows. *Susanne Lachenicht's* contribution makes evident that neither hosting societies nor the gate-keepers (or religious and administrative elites) of the Sephardi Diaspora tolerated individual Portuguese Jews' flexible attitudes towards national identity. However, both the *converso* experience in Portugal and in Diaspora and the economic, social and political needs of both members of the rising Portuguese Jewish Diaspora and the hosting societies hindered the formation of clearly separate communities.

For the Huguenots *Bertrand Van Ruymbeke* finds that the flight of 150,000 to 200,000 French Protestants, following the revocation of the Edict of Nantes (1685), enhanced the formation of a French Protestant nation abroad. Nonetheless, their integration into the host societies emphasised a »chameleon faculty to blend in various cultural environments« which finally led to assimilation.

Moving from the early modern to the modern period, *Maurizio Isabella* argues that European nationalisms of the nineteenth century evolved in cosmopolitan contexts of exile such as Brussels, Paris and London. This »accounts for the intimate connection between the various patriotisms [...] and for the existence of shared values, principles and discursive patterns among patriots of different national origins« and »produced brands of nationalism that reconciled national with universal claims«. A strong uniting element was the merging of faith, political freedom and progress with religion, individual rights and ideas of nationhood. While some patriots opted for a new patriotic religion, others, such as Vincenzo Gioberti or

Adam Mickiewicz, found Catholicism as being at the very heart of the character of the Italian or Polish nations. Nineteenth century nationalisms inherited the French revolutionary sacralisation of politics, but also gave rise to the re-birth of old religions translated into the needs of leading European patriots. They re-interpreted early modern concepts of religious minorities such as martyrdom. Also, political exile became a pilgrimage, no longer for the religious faith alone but, mainly, for the fatherland. Compared to the French Calvinists' or Huguenots' national identities, which combined French patriotism and the myth of being the very best that France had to offer with their being their being God's elect (Lachenicht 2007), nineteenth century nationalisms seem to owe more to early modern nationalisms, as they evolved in diaspora, than research has suggested so far.

Frank Grüner demonstrates in his *Nationalism and anti-Cosmopolitanism in Russian Radical Right and Soviet Ideology* that anti-cosmopolitanism, identified as an anti-Semitic and anti-modernisation ideology, was rooted not only in the pre-Soviet Russian Radical Right but in Russian society. When Stalin revived anti-cosmopolitanism after the Second World War, he drew on long-established traditions that enabled him to mobilise large parts of the Soviet society for an anti-western and anti-Semitic orientation in ideology. While from a modern western perspective cosmopolitanism is identified as a positive value, the Russian and Soviet context shows that this is not universal. In a historical perspective, cosmopolitan attitudes of exiles and diaspora communities, as Grüner shows, decried, more often than not, their patriotism for the hosting state. Anti-cosmopolitanism served as a powerful ideology to justify persecution and, finally, the elimination of minority groups.

Anna Holian moves beyond the period of extreme nationalisms in *Between Nationalism and Internationalism: Displaced Persons at the UNRRA University of Munich*. The UNRRA's sponsors attempted to re-introduce humanist (which included cosmopolitan) values in an environment where protagonists and victims of nationalist and National Socialist ideologies met. The UNRRA University was an »Erziehungsstätte zum Weltbürgertum«. Anna Holian shows how the tension between a »liberal internationalism« and a »cosmopolitan internationalism« challenged nationalisms as typical of many displaced persons studying at UNRRA. While the »liberal internationalism« envisioned »the world as a community of nations in which each nation can be seen internally united and externally differentiated, and in which individuals appear as representatives of given nations«, the UNRRA's »cosmopolitan internationalism« saw »the world as a community of individual world citizens, in which differences of nationality do not come into play and may in fact be transcended«.

With her study of Eva Reichmann, *Kirsten Heinsohn* traces a Diaspora biography rooted in liberal Judaism combined with affinities to Zionism. Before her flight to England in 1939, religion, her Jewishness, and her German nationality formed a Jewish German identity of the 1920s and early 1930s. In exile, however, Eva Reichmann developed cosmopolitan and universalist ideas and attempted to reconcile them with her being a German national and a Jewish woman. In her eyes, the nullification of the emancipation of German Jews required new approaches to Diaspora. It was »to countervail an exaggerated nationalism« and to become an »intellectual-spiritual path«, a concept that the Boyarin seem to echo. The new Jewish homeland and the Diaspora became essential poles for the creation of Jewish identities, which had an ethnic and religious origin, just as the Sephardi Jews or French Huguenots.

Kate Daniels describes in *»The Song of Everyone without a Homeland«: Mahmud Darwish in »Cosmopolitan« Beirut* cosmopolitanism as an ideal and as attitudes typical of exile. In close contact with the competing Lebanese and Palestinian nationalisms, between sects, ethnicities, political parties and factions, Darwish developed universalising humanist visions of cosmopolitanism »in spite of – if not *because of* – his narrower priorities of Palestinian return and self-determination«. Mahmud Darwish saw »no inherent contradiction between his engaging with the human cultural legacy in its entirety and his foregrounding of the Palestinian cultural tradition« and does not »descend into immoderate chauvinism or exclusive nationalist sentiment«.

We hope that this volume will inspire discussions, a new dialogue and new perspectives on the interrelatedness of exile (or diasporas), nationalism and cosmopolitanism in a historical perspective. We do not provide *one* definition of nationalism and cosmopolitanism or offer a model of how these interact in situations of exile or diaspora. Nor do we suggest a linear process of how concepts of nation, nationalisms and cosmopolitanism evolved over time and space. However, some conclusions can be drawn:

Cosmopolitanism has to be identified as both an idea (or ideal) and as practices or attitudes. The latter are often as important for the economic and political survival of diasporas as the formation of a distinct national identity. Cosmopolitanism as an idea can structure elite networks such as humanist correspondence or the Republic of Letters and the Enlightenment. Internationalist and cosmopolitan attitudes and ideas can also be inherent to religion (Catholicism, Islam) and political ideologies (socialism). However, even with universalist phenomena such as religion and ideologies, cosmopolitan attitudes and practices co-exist more often than not with nationalism and national exclusiveness. For situations of exile and diaspora this has been illustrated by early modern examples such as the Irish Catholic, the Sephardi or the Huguenot diasporas as much as by modern case-studies of the UNRRA-University or the biography of Mahmud Darwish.

Nations in exile or diasporic groups chose survival strategies which are both nationalist and cosmopolitan. While establishing economic and intellectual networks that have always been identified as cosmopolitan, diaspora communities intend to form distinct communities and nations. Situations of exile and diaspora can enhance the formation of distinct national identities which might not have been formed in the homeland, as the examples of the Sephardim, the Huguenots and protagonists of the Italian *Risorgimento* suggest.

Cosmopolitanism has often been regarded as a negative attitude, as being antagonistic to national interests, both for nations at home and nations abroad, that is diasporas without a homeland. This is true for the Sephardim, the Huguenots and the Russian or Soviet context. Cosmopolitan attitudes and ideas are not related to specific historical periods. Whether they are supposed to have a positive or negative impact on states, the economy and societies depends on historical specificity: traumatic periods such as the first half of the twentieth century, marked by totalitarian states, can enhance a growing desire for universal humanist values and ethical norms.

Exile and diasporas are »hotbeds« for nationalism, internationalism and cosmopolitanism. Up-rootedness, being discriminated against by the hosting societies and the need to redefine one's own identity entail a stronger consciousness of (national) identity. They also increase the desire to protect and safeguard this identity and to relocate it in a distinct territory. Diasporas, too, can satisfy these needs, and ensure that a group's identity survive (as the example of the Huguenots or the Sephardim shows). Exile and diaspora can be spheres of creativity. They can also be places of discrimination, racism and pathological struggles between nations and ethnic and/or religious groups (Cohen 1997).

While it has often been suggested that, in the early modern period, religion had played a more important role in shaping exclusive identities than ethnicity, this volume makes evident that this has to be nuanced. Clearly, the lost homeland became part of the sacred; with the French Revolution, Christian religions seem to have been replaced by patriotism and nationalism. However, sacrifices on the altar of the *patria* never fully replaced the role of religion for national identities, such as Anglicanism in England or Catholicism in Italy or Spain. Especially for modern nationalisms arising in modern diasporas religion played and still plays an eminent role.

We must distinguish between nationalism and cosmopolitanism as ideas, ideals, attitudes, labels and strategies of survival of individuals and groups in order to analyse how they intertwine and interact. In the context of exile, nationalism and cosmopolitanism are not related linearly but in a dialectic tension, different in each individual context. And both nationalism and cosmopolitanism should be categories of and for analysis.

Several of the following contributions were first presented at an international meeting in Hamburg, June 2007, which was generously funded by the Fritz-Thyssen-Stiftung.

Works cited

Archibugi, Daniele (ed.). (2003). *Debating Cosmopolitics*. London: Verso.

Beck, Ulrich (2004). *Der kosmopolitische Blick, oder: Krieg ist Frieden*. Frankfurt/Main: Suhrkamp.

Beck, Ulrich and Edgar Grande (2004). *Das kosmopolitische Europa. Gesellschaft und Politik in der Zweiten Moderne*. Frankfurt/Main: Suhrkamp.

Berlin, Ira (2003). *Generations of Captivity: A History of African-American Slaves*. Cambridge: Harvard University Press.

Bloxham, Donald (2005). *The Great Game of Genocide: Imperialism, Nationalism, and the Destruction of the Ottoman Armenians*. Oxford: Oxford University Press.

Boyarin, Daniel and Jonathan (1993). Diaspora: generation and the ground of Jewish identity. *Critical Enquiry* 19/4, 693–725.

Cheah, Pheng and Bruce Robbins (eds.). (1998). *Cosmopolitics. Thinking and Feeling beyond the Nation*. Minneapolis, London: University of Minnesota Press.

Clifford, James (1994). Diasporas. *Current Anthropology*, 9 (3), 302–338.

Cohen, Robin (1997). *Global Diasporas: An Introduction*. Seattle: University of Washington Press.

Davis, Todd F. and Kenneth Womack (eds.). (2001). *Mapping the Ethical Turn. A Reader in Ethics, Culture and Literary Theory*. Charlottesville: University of Virginia Press.

Dickason, Olive Patricia (1997). *Canada's First Nations: A History of Founding Peoples from Earliest Times*. Toronto: Oxford University Press.

Gallois, William (2008). *The Administration of Sickness: Medicine and Ethics in Colonial Algeria*. Basingstoke: Palgrave Macmillan.

Kaldor, Mary (1996). Cosmopolitanism versus Nationalism: The New Divide? In Richard Caplan and John Feffer (eds.). *Europe's New Nationalism. States and Minorities in Conflict*, 42–58. Oxford, New York: Oxford University Press.

Kleingeld, Pauline and Eric Brown. Cosmopolitanism. For *Stanford Encyclopedia of Philosophy*, http://plato.stanford.edu, 2006 (revised and updated version of 2002 entry). Accessed 4 April 2009.

Lachenicht, Susanne (2007). Huguenot Immigrants and the Formation of National Identities, *The Historical Journal*, 50/2, 309–331.

Lubkoll, Christine and Oda Wischmeyer (eds.). (2009). *Ethical Turn? Geisteswissenschaften in neuer Verantwortung*. Paderborn: Fink.

Lutz, John Sutton (ed.). (2007). *Myth and Memory: Stories of Indigenous-European Contact*. Vancouver: University of British Columbia Press.

Nussbaum, Martha C. (1996). Patriotism and Cosmopolitanism. In Martha C. Nussbaum and Joshua Cohen (eds.). *For love of Country: Debating the Limits of Patriotism*, 3–20. Boston: Beacon Press.

Nussbaum, Martha C. and Joshua Cohen (eds.). (1996). *For love of Country: Debating the Limits of Patriotism*. Boston: Beacon Press

Rosenfeld, Michel (2006). Derrida's Ethical Turn and America: Looking Back from the Crossroads of Global Terrorism and the Enlightenment. *Cardozo Law Review*, 27, 815–846.

Shustermann, R. (1993). Next year in Jerusalem: postmodern Jewish identity and the myth of return. In T.D. Goldberg and M. Krausz (eds.). *Jewish Identity*, 291–308. Philadelphia: Temple University Press.

Thompson, Alvin O. (2006). *Flight to Freedom: African Runaways and Maroons in the Americas*. Mona: University of West Indies Press.

Vertovec, Steven and Robin Cohen (eds.). (2002). *Conceiving Cosmopolitanism: Theory, Context, and Practice*. Oxford: Oxford University Press.

»*Une Seconde Patrie*«: The Irish Colleges, Paris, in the Eighteenth and Nineteenth Centuries[1]

Liam Chambers

The large-scale migration of Irish Catholics to continental Europe commenced in the later sixteenth century and continued until the 1790s. The expansion of English administrative and military control across the island of Ireland, combined with attempts to bring the Protestant reformation to the country, created military conflict, political upheaval and intermittent religious persecution which necessitated or encouraged emigration. In addition, Ireland's peripheral geographical location ensured that during periods of economic hardship people looked to opportunities abroad. Mass migration, which involved thousands of people, coincided with the successive military defeats of Irish Catholics and their allies in 1602-3, the 1650s and 1690-1. However, steady migration also occurred throughout the seventeenth and eighteenth centuries, though the number of people migrating to continental Europe was already deceasing by the 1750s and the decline continued into the later eighteenth century. Migration from Ireland to the continent was overwhelmingly Catholic. While it was socially diverse, a number of categories of migrants stand out. Thousands of Irish soldiers enlisted abroad, many of them in the Irish regiments established in the French and Spanish armies. Merchants and traders established bases in ports along the western Atlantic seaboard. During periods of persecution Irish clergy sought refuge in Catholic states on the continent and, from the late sixteenth century, many students resided at more than thirty Irish Colleges, which emerged in the leading centres of Catholic education in France, Spain, the Low Countries, the Italian states and beyond. (Cullen 1994; O'Connor 2001, 2001a; O'Connor and Lyons 2003, 2006).

---

1 This essay draws, in part, on material discussed in more detail in Chambers 2009, forthcoming.

The Irish Colleges emerged in response to the needs of the communities of Irish Catholic students which had sprung up in European university towns in the later sixteenth century. Their founders wished to facilitate the education of students for whom higher educational opportunities were unavailable in Ireland (or England and Scotland). This was especially pressing as the Catholic church re-organised and re-structured in Ireland. Most colleges were therefore established by Catholic clergy, with the intention of forming well-educated priests capable of taking their place on the Irish mission. In reality the colleges fulfilled a range of functions as student hostels, university colleges, lay boarding schools, monastic establishments and seminaries. Most colleges were small, catering for less than twenty students, though there were exceptions such as Paris, where two colleges catered for 180 students by the 1780s. Among the students were ordained priests, as well as younger unordained students, some of them destined for ordination, others for secular careers. The number of staff was usually relatively small, though this was related to the provision of education within the colleges. Many of the Irish Colleges were not educational institutions in their own right. Students attended classes and took degrees at a local university or college. Only a small number of colleges, notably those of the regular clergy, provided courses in humanities, philosophy and theology. Even where colleges were not directly responsible for the provision of lectures, they provided a controlled environment, where discipline was imposed and (ideally at least) opinions were monitored, though a detailed daily timetable, spiritual exercises, instruction in the Irish language and, in some cases, extra lectures. In this sense, the colleges were responsible for much of the formation of the Irish Catholic cultural elite, clerical and lay, and comprised an integral aspect of Irish Catholic culture in the early modern period. Indeed, they also played an important role in the development of Irish communities in continental towns. The colleges were obvious focal points and some provided a range of services to expanding Irish communities: the staff and students assisted the destitute, invested money on behalf of soldiers and others, provided legal advice and assistance (for example, in the drawing up of wills), translated documents and produced attestations of identity. Moreover, not all students or priests returned to the Irish mission on the completion of their studies. A large proportion chose to remain on the continent, many of whom ministered to the Irish Catholic migrant communities. As Irish migration to Europe declined significantly in the late eighteenth century (re-orienting across the Atlantic and into the British Empire), the colleges encountered serious difficulties. Almost all of the colleges closed as a result of the French Revolution and its continental impact. A few re-emerged in the early nineteenth century, at Rome, Salamanca, Lisbon and – especially – Paris. An

Irish College in Paris continued to function as an educational institution until 1939

The Irish Colleges have not lacked historians, especially during a »golden age« of Irish ecclesiastical history in the late nineteenth and early twentieth centuries when the survival of Irish Catholicism in the early modern period was ascribed in large part to their influence. A more sophisticated analysis of the colleges has emerged only in the past few decades as Irish, English and other European historians have waded more deeply in continental archives. This work is placing the colleges more firmly within Irish migrant networks and the social, political and religious fabric of their host communities (O'Boyle 1935; Walsh 1973; Boyle 1901; Swords 1978, 1980; Brockliss and Ferté 1987, 2004; O'Connor 2006; Chambers 2006). In tandem with other developments in Irish history, recent work has also renewed interest in the connections between Irish Catholic migration to Europe, especially before 1789, and the construction of Irish national identities (McBride 2001; Mac Cana 2001). This article considers how the Irish Colleges in Paris negotiated identity in the eighteenth and nineteenth centuries. It argues that the experience of exile, or migration, or simply living abroad for an extended period, both encouraged the development of an Irish identity and produced a fluid and adaptable approach to identity necessary for survival and success.

Though the Irish Colleges established in the late sixteenth and seventeenth centuries asserted a clear national identity, as »Irish« Colleges, during the early phase of their existence, from the late sixteenth century to the mid-to-late seventeenth century, there was a constant tension between the »national« claims and the provincial realities. It is not surprising that the nascent colleges reflected the ethnic and provincial divisions which marked Irish Catholicism, socially and politically, during this period (Walsh 1973, 14–15). The Irish Colleges in Paris initially fitted this pattern, i.e., laying claim to an »Irish« identity, but in reality linked most closely migrant students from Leinster (O'Connor 2006, 10–56). By the middle of the seventeenth century, however, Paris was attracting a diverse range of students from Ireland, cutting across ethnic and provincial lines, so that by the time a permanent Irish College (the *Collège des Lombards*) was established in the city in the 1670s, it could realistically claim to be a national Irish college, and regulations were drawn up in 1670s and 1680s which guaranteed this »national« character (Swords 1980, 28–32). During the eighteenth century the Irish College in Paris became by far the most important institution of its kind and a second permanent college opened in the city in the 1770s (Swords 1980, 4).

In the early seventeenth century leading figures associated with the Irish College in Paris were developing ideological and cultural responses to the political and military setbacks suffered by Irish Catholicism. Thomas O'Connor has illustrated how the early superior of the Irish College in Paris, Thomas Messingham, played a key role in the creation and promotion of an Irish Catholic nationality for a European audience (O'Connor 1999). In a sermon preached at the college in 1620, his colleague David Rothe emphasised the need to bury divisions in favour of a common Irish identity (Rothe 1620, 124–49). In the eighteenth century, a group of scholars associated with the college produced a series of important and influential works on the Irish language and Irish history. These included Irish language dictionaries published in the 1730s and 1760s and a bi-lingual Irish-English Catechism published in the 1740s ([Begley and MacCurtain] 1732; Donlevy 1742; O'Brien 1768). They also included David Henegan's historical writings on Ireland, published in the 1759 edition of Moreri's *Dictionnaire*, and Abbé James McGeoghegan's three-volume *Histoire d'Irlande* published in the late 1750s and early 1760s (Henegan 1759; MacGeoghegan 1758–62; Geoghegan 1991). Together, these works illustrate the important role of migrant scholars in the development of an Irish Catholic national identity in the eighteenth century. That the experience of migration influenced their writings is clear. James MacGeoghegan, for example, pitched his *Histoire* directly at an *émigré* Irish (as well as a French) readership.

However, the peculiar position of the Irish Colleges in Paris fostered an adaptable approach to identity, which encompassed Irish, French and British aspects. This adaptability is revealed by the response of the college authorities to moments of crisis, especially in the late eighteenth and early nineteenth centuries. One response to crisis was closely linked to the promotion of the Irish language and historical scholarship, and emphasised the distinctive Irish and foreign identity of the colleges. In 1762–1763 the Irish *Collège des Lombards* was threatened with amalgamation into the *Collège Louis-le-Grand*, from which the Jesuits had been expelled in 1762 (Tuilier 1994, 161–74). The administrators (*proviseurs*) argued forcefully against amalgamation, rooting their case on the distinct nature of the Irish Colleges from the other colleges and student bodies within the university. The main petition highlighted:

»Leur nombre, leur langage, leurs moeurs, leur façon de vivre et de se nourrir, le genre d'étude, qui est leur particulier, la nécessité de conserver des supérieurs tirés de leur nation, le peu de resource, enfin, que l'on trouveroit dans la location de leurs bâtimens pour améliorer leur condition sont des raisons dont chacune, en particulier, semble former un obstacle invincible à leur reunion avec les boursiers des autres colleges.«[2]

For these reasons, continued the petition, the college should form »une maison particulière et isolée«.[3] The administrators also drew on the »extremely severe« penal laws in Ireland (though these were largely ignored by the 1760s) to make their case. The image of persecuted Irish Catholics remained an important rhetorical device long after it had ceased to exist in reality.[4] In 1763 the administrators' argument was successful and the college was exempted from the proposed amalgamation (Amadou 1986, 37–8). But this very success in maintaining institutional autonomy now meant that the college stood out as a clear anomaly. As Mike Rapport has pointed out in relation to the Scots College in Paris, which used a very similar tactic in the 1760s and was also successful in retaining institutional autonomy, the very factor which saved the college in the 1760s became a liability in the 1790s (Rapport 2002, 81–4).

In fact, the Irish Colleges were firmly embedded within the educational, ecclesiastical and political fabric of eighteenth century Paris and they (and the Irish student population more generally) had no difficulty in expressing a form of French identity or »attachment« when this was required. When the reputation of a group of Irish students resident at the *Collège des Grassins* was attacked by college and university authorities in 1710, the students published a *Mémoire* which carefully outlined the service of former students and related family members to both the French army and the Irish Catholic mission, consciously linking the two (Anon. 1710; Boyle 1901a). When the Irish college in Paris was in severe financial difficulties in the 1780s, the superior, John Baptist Walsh, penned a *Mémoire* to solicit funds from potential French patrons. In this case, Walsh stressed the value and attachment of the college to France: supplying chaplains to the Irish and other regiments in the French army, priests to the French church and service to

2 »Mémoire pour le Collège des Lombards«, 24 November 1762 (Archives Nationales, H3 2561B, Collège des Irlandais: Historique, lettres patentes, pieces diverses, 1623 to XVIIIe siècle).

3 Ibid.

4 »Addition au Memoire du College des Lombards«, undated, with attachment: »Extrait di Recueil des Loix d'Irlande« (Ibid.).

the French state. Similar sentiments are evident after 1789.[5] In December 1790 a group of Irish students were arrested following a fracas at the Altar of the Fatherland on the Champ de Mars (Swords 1989, 31–6). Predictably, they were quickly denounced as counter-revolutionaries by some radical pamphleteers, who highlighted the fact that they were foreign, though they failed to identify the students as Irish. However, a number of pamphlets appeared which defended the Irish. One work, signed by a member of the »Club de Cordeliers« is particularly revealing. It argued that the Irish were, in fact, good patriots: »Français par reconnaissance, Français par attachement, Français par intétêt, comme propriétaires, comment pourroient-ils, ces Irlandois, chercher à être odieux à la nation Françoise.« (Anon. 1790a, 3) Another pamphleteer drew on the heritage of Franco-Irish connections: »Ce sont des Irlandois qui se font remarquer dans tous le pays par leur attachment pour la France; *qui, de tout temps, ont chéri la France comme une seconde patrie.*« (Anon. [1790], 4, my italics) After two weeks in prison, the students were tried for disfiguring the altar of the fatherland and attacking the sentinel and were acquitted. It is interesting that the students were referred to as »English« not Irish in the judgement.[6] Perhaps the most significant point about the incident is the means of defence available to the Irish. Their defence cast them as good French patriots and saw no contradiction in highlighting simultaneously their Irish and French identities. In this they reflected the arguments developed by college administrators in 1789–90.

During the early French Revolution, the Irish College administrators (who were probably behind the pamphlets cited above) saw no contradiction in simultaneously projecting Irish and the French identities. Indeed, the cosmopolitanism of the early Revolution encouraged this outlook and helps to explain the tactics used by the Irish Colleges as the structures of higher education (within which the colleges were firmly embedded) were dismantled. In the face of this threat the Irish College administrators amalgamated two positions – that the Irish Colleges were »distinct« institutions and that the Irish students were essentially French, at least by »attachment« – to produce a Franco-Irish anti-Britishness that suited the political climate of the early 1790s. This position was clearly articulated in a petition penned by John Baptist Walsh to the ecclesiastical committee of the National As-

5 Mémoire ([Paris], 1787) (A.N., T 1636, Papiers séquestrés, Collège des Lombards et Collège des Irlandais).

6 The subsequent legal proceedings detail the case: A.N. F7 4624 (plaq. 4), ff 182–212.

sembly requesting exemption from the nationalisation of ecclesiastical property (Swords 1989, 22–9). Walsh argued that the majority Irish Catholic population was antipathetic to the government. Indeed they were comparable with the Revolutionary French: »[Ils] sentiront les droits et la dignité de l'homme et ils secouront le joug d'un pareil esclavage.« (Daumet 1912, 202)[7] For this reason, Ireland afforded France an opportunity to enhance its international standing in relation to Britain: »N'en doutons pas, si cette isle devenoit indépendante de l'Angleterre, la France n'auroit plus rien a redoubter de sa rivalle qui sera humiliée sans coup férir.« (ibid.) On this basis (a shared anti-Britishness), Walsh argued, the French Revolutionaries ought to maintain the Irish Colleges:

> »Le gouvernement anglois déteste la Révolution que rénénère la France et il fera tous ses efforts pour empêcher les étudians irlandois et venire puiser dans nos écoles les principes qui feront tôt ou tard éclore le germe de la liberté si naturelle aux hommes.
>
> La France est donc intéressée par humanité et par une saine politique à conserver les maisons étrangères, sans parler du lustre et de la gloire de devenir le centre et l'Athènes des sciences.« (Ibid.).

In a second petition, Walsh drew on the service of the Irish Colleges to France, which he had outlined before the Revolution. Moreover, he argued emphatically that the Irish Colleges did not require the assistance of the British ambassador in Paris, unlike their colleagues in the Scots College (Ibid. 204–5; Rapport 2002, 85–8). A third petition, to the National Assembly (seeking confirmation of a decision by the Ecclesiastical Committee to exempt the Irish Colleges) pushed the arguments even further:

> »Le supérieur a l'honneur d'observer que cette maison n'a rien de commun soit avec les religieux étrangers quelconques, soit avec MM. les Ecossois ou Anglois de Paris. Ceux-ci sollicitent la permission de vendre pour quitter la France. Au contraire, les Irlandois demandent à s'y attacher de plus en plus.
>
> Le Comité est donc supplié de prendre en consideration *le nombre, l'utilité et le civisme des prêtres irlandois étudians en France* et de poser la base de leur tranquilité en faisant decreter promptement la conservation de leur maison principale dans le Collège des Lombards.« (Daumet 1912, 205).

The exemption, which ensured the short-term future of the college, was duly confirmed in October 1790 (Anon. 1790b).

7 Daumet (1912) printed Walsh's first two mémoires (pp 201–4). The original documents are in A.N. D XIX 30, liasse 472 (Comité Ecclésiastique).

Of course, recognising this pragmatic approach to identity politics does not imply that the Irish College authorities were ardent revolutionaries. In fact, while they proclaimed their revolutionary credentials when appropriate, they also facilitated the development of a refractory church network in the Faubourg Saint-Marcel (Chambers 2009; Burstin 2005, 211–45, 667–76). As the Revolution passed from the early moderate phase to the Terror, it became increasingly difficult, if not impossible, for the Irish College authorities and students to present themselves as Irish *and* French, revolutionary and refractory. As Mike Rapport has argued »the French Revolution [...] made citizenship dependant on nationality« (Rapport 2000, 333). In consequence, foreigners had to abandon other allegiances in order to be members of the French nation and thereby to exercise political rights. This placed foreign clergy in a particularly difficult situation.

As foreign and ecclesiastical institutions it is remarkable that the Irish Colleges remained open until 1793, when the war with Great Britain finally resulted in their closure. Elsewhere in France and across Europe, the Irish Colleges were affected by the Revolution. Most closed and would not re-open after the dust finally settled. In Paris, the colleges were returned to Irish control in 1795, but the damage inflicted since 1793 and the collapse of student migration from Ireland meant an uncertain future (Swords 1989, 82–106). However, the value of the properties and the lucrative investments attached to the colleges ensured that there was keen interest in reviving them. From the later 1790s until the 1820s there ensued a battle for control between two key Irish groups. The »secular group« favoured the Revolution and wanted to transform the college into a Franco-Irish institution for the education of the children of *émigrés* sympathetic to the revolution and to remove Irish clerical and Episcopal influence. In the ascendancy during the early 1810s, this group remained influential until the early 1820s (Purcell 1985). In the long term, however, the other side of the struggle emerged victorious. This »clerical group« were antagonistic towards the Revolution, viewed the college as an Irish Catholic ecclesiastical institution and envisaged it as an Irish seminary.[8] This group found it in-

8 The pre-1789 administrators of the Irish Colleges played an important role in this respect, though both John Baptist Walsh and Charles Kearney were willing to compromise with the Napoleonic regime in order to secure the future of the colleges. After 1814, Paul Long emerged as the key figure. For Walsh and Kearney see: Swords 1989; Boyle 1905, 1908. There is, as yet, no satisfactory study of the role of Paul Long, which emerges in his correspondence with Dublin: Dublin Diocesan Archives

creasingly difficult to reconcile their Irish Catholic identity with attachment to France. In response, they began to engage with a new British sense of identity the early nineteenth century. This is particularly evident in the correspondence of Paul Long, a Dublin priest who was dispatched to Paris by the Irish bishops in 1814 to take charge of the sole Irish College to re-open in Paris and to assert the claims of the Irish bishops. Long, who had studied in Paris before the French Revolution, was deeply pessimistic about its effects. In a letter written in September 1815 he commented:

»Such are the fruits of the Revolution, that the four-fifths of Frenchmen can be considered as Atheists, or Deists, and the greater number of the remaining fifth as merely nominal Catholics. The clergy of course are held in no estimation; they are ranked with the lowest class of society, are reviled on every occasion, and almost entirely excluded from what is termed genteel society.«[9]

As a result, he urged the Irish bishops »to sell the property, and transfer the price to Ireland. There is no longer any security for our property in this kingdom«.[10]

There were other factors which facilitated Long's assertion of the »British« identity of the college. In the 1790s the British government and the Irish Catholic bishops had formed an alliance, against the Revolutionary threat which horrified them both. One important consequence was the foundation of a third-level Catholic college at Maynooth, in Ireland, which undermined the importance of the Irish Colleges on the continent as formation centres for well-educated Irish Catholic clergy (Keogh 1993, 1–88) However, in the early nineteenth century the Catholic population in Ireland was growing rapidly and the Irish bishops therefore realised the importance of re-opening the recently constructed Irish College in Paris and re-establishing Irish Catholic claims to the investments made in scholarships at the Irish and other colleges attached to the University of Paris over more than a century.[11] In response to requests made by John Baptist Walsh, proviseur of the Irish *Collège des Lombards* on the outbreak of the Revolution and a key figure behind its survival during the Revolutionary and Napoleonic periods, and similar appeals from those charged with the

---

DDA/AB3/34/17, Papers of Archbishop Daniel Murray: Irish College Paris Part 2 (1814–1853).

9 Paul Long to Dr Hamill, 5 September 1815 (DDA/AB3/34/17/161)

10 Ibid.

11 See for example, Paul Long to Bishop Daniel Murray, 17 February 1815 (DDA/AB3/34/17/153).

affairs of the Scots and English Colleges in Paris, Napoleon made an unexpected decision. In 1802 and 1803 he ordered the amalgamation of all the Irish, English and Scots institutions under his jurisdiction into a singe entity called the »British Establishments«. This was done against the wishes of the Irish, Scots and English authorities in Paris and Ireland, Scotland and England. However, the Irish were by far the largest of the three groups and while they were not keen on the arrangement, John Baptist Walsh ensured that he was appointed as administrator of the new »British establishments« and used the situation to re-open the *Collège des Irlandais* to Irish, English and Scots, as well as some French, students in 1805. Napoleon's willingness to re-open the Irish College, albeit as part of the »British Establishments« was predicated on the establishment of a French *bureau*, charged with oversight of the college. This was done in response to the vacuum left by the collapse of the *ancien régime* structures within which the colleges had functioned (Swords 1989, 160–74).

In 1816 the government of Louis XVIII finally ended the unhappy marriage of the Irish, Scots and English Colleges.[12] However, the French *bureau* remained, which ensured that the Irish College looked to Britain for protection against the alleged encroachments of the French government, especially after 1814 when the college was increasingly under the control of the »clerical« faction. By this stage there was another practical reason for expressing a sense of British identity. Paul Long hoped that he could recover compensation for the losses suffered by the Irish College during the 1790s. This possibility was offered by the second treaty of Paris, which stipulated *inter alia* that British subjects would be indemnified for properties or investments lost after 1 January 1791 and that a commission would be established to assess claims (Anon. 1815). Between his arrival in France in 1814 and the end of his mission in 1819, Long wrote regular and generally pessimistic accounts of his affairs back to Bishop Daniel Murray in Dublin. While the establishment of a commission promised the return of investments lost during the 1790s, which would put the college back on a secure financial basis, Long quickly ran into problems. In April 1817 Long explained to Murray, that French government officials were arguing that the Irish Colleges had been established contrary to British law and were therefore not encompassed within the agreement:

12 Long to Troy, 30 January 1816 (DDA/AB3/34/17/uncalendared item).

»Nothing can be done here [i.e. in France]. The matter must evidently be settled in London. It is therefore of the highest importance to our interests to endeavour to induce Lord Castlereagh [the Irish-born British Foreign Secretary] to consider our property here as British property, being purchased by British subjects, with British money, & to give orders accordingly to the English commissioners in Paris.«[13]

A few months later, in July 1817, Long explained the position again:

»The validity of the objection, raised against our claims by the French government, being once admitted by the English cabinet, all hope of indemnity for past losses is totally destroyed; our houses are no longer Irish but French institutions, & we remain involved in the same general and irreparable misfortune. However it is very difficult to conceive for what manner establishments formed by and for British subjects with British money can be viewed in this light.«[14]

Rooted in pragmatic considerations, especially concerns about the level of French government interference, the Irish College administrators and the Irish bishops looked to the British government for protection. In 1818 Bishop Murray of Dublin sought the assistance of Sir Charles Stuart, the British ambassador in Paris, stressing that the Irish College was an Irish establishment not a French one.[15] Despite this approach, in 1825 a British Commission established to assess claims for losses during the French Revolution finally rejected the Irish College's claims, despite the assertion of a British identity.[16] The possibility of re-activating the claim (especially around 1830 and again in the 1870s) ensured that this British identity remained (Historicus Hibernicus 1870; *Claims* 1871). More generally, throughout the nineteenth century, the Irish Colleges could use their British connection to protect the institution, especially when the college was seriously threatened.

The point is that the collapse of the French »attachment« or identity of the Irish Colleges, and its administrators and students, facilitated the expression of »Britishness«, however pragmatic this may have been. This underlines how adaptable the Irish Colleges were: Irish, French, »Franco-Irish«, anti-British and even British. However, as the nineteenth century progressed the Irish College, increasingly distanced from Parisian and

13 Long to Murray, 26 April 1817 (DDA/AB3/34/17/188).

14 Long to Murray, 20 July 1817 (DDA/AB3/34/17/190).

15 [Murray] »A son excellence Sir Charles Stuart Ambassador de Sa Majésté Britannique près la Cour de France« (copy; c. 1 April 1818) (DDA/AB3/34/17/210).

16 Charles Baldwin to Paul Long, 2 Dec. 1825 (copy dated 1 March 1830) (Archives of the Irish College, Paris, MS 3.O).

French culture, more clearly identified itself simply as »Irish«. There are a number of significant reasons for this. In the nineteenth century the Irish College no longer formed part of a large Irish migrant community in Paris, as had been the case in the *ancien régime*. The growing secularisation of French politics and society, especially during the Third Republic had a profound effect on the college. Threatened with closure and confiscation after 1905, the superior of the college wrote tellingly: »If, therefore, France closes the college and retains the capital, she violates the intentions of the founders, she strikes a blow at the rights of aliens all over the world. She inflicts a wrong on a nation which in the past looked to France as a friend and protector.« (Boyle 1907, 298) The increasing remoteness of the Irish College from French society co-incided with the rise of Irish cultural nationalism. The Irish College was not a hotbed of revolutionary activity, but it participated in the development of nationalism. Irish language studies were re-introduced at the college from the middle of the nineteenth century. Students at the Irish College responded enthusiastically to the visit of the radical Irish nationalist John Mitchell in 1866 (Swords 1985, unpaginated). The nationalist influence is also evident in the Celtic Revival art and architecture promoted (ironically) by the French administrator of the college from 1859, Abbé Charles Ouin LaCroix (McDonnell 2002).

The experience of migration (exile is probably too strong) encouraged Irish Catholic students and priests associated with the Irish Colleges in Paris to develop an Irish Catholic identity in the early modern period. However, the experience of migration also fostered an adaptable approach to »identity«, one which permitted the Irish Colleges to emphasise their French-ness or French »attachment«. Like the wider Irish migrant community, this encouraged assimilation and the permanent migration of priests and students, though they were theoretically destined to return to Ireland. The rupture of the French Revolution and the rise of nineteenth century cultural nationalism contributed to the emergence of an Irish College which was more remote from the society around it, one which was increasingly an outpost of Irish Catholicism. Yet, even in the nineteenth century the practical problems of maintaining an »Irish« College in a foreign country meant that the college could balance its Irish nationalist sympathies with a pragmatic Britishness. Irish, French and British identities were, of course, themselves malleable and contested throughout the eighteenth and nineteenth centuries. However, the long term approach taken by the present essay suggests that the success (or longevity) of the Irish College(s) in Paris may, in part, be attributed to an adaptable and flexible approach to identity, fostered by the experience of migration.

Works cited

Anon. (1790a). *Adresse au peuple de la capital, sur l'événement du Champ de Mars, le lundi 6 décembre 1790.* Paris: De Chalon.

Anon. (1790b). *Loi relative aux établissemens d'études, d'enseignemens, ou simplement religieux, faits en France par des étrangers, & pour eux memes. Donné à Paris, le 7 november 1790.* Paris: no publisher.

Anon. (1790c). *Justification des écoliers irlandais, sur l'événement qui s'est passé au Champ de Mars, le lundi six du mois.* Paris: no publisher.

Anon. (1710). *Mémoire Exact et Véritable du Nombre des Officiers Irlandais qui ont été élevez dans la Fondation de feu l'Abbé Patrice Maginn.* No place of publication, no publisher.

Anon. (1815). *Traité et Conventions entre le Roi et les Puissances Alliées conclus à Paris le 20 Novembre 1815.* Paris: Impr. Royale.

Anon. (1871). *Claims of the Irish College Paris on the British Government, in virtue of treaties with France.* Cork: J. Mahony & Son.

Amadou, Robert (1986). Saint-Ephrem Des Syriens du Collège des Lombards à nos jours. *Mémoires de la Féderation des sociétés historiques et archéologiques de Paris et l'Ile de France*, 37, 6–152.

[Begley ,Abbé and Hugh MacCurtain] (1732). *The English Irish dictionary: An focloir bearla Gaoidheilge. Ar na chur a neagar le Conchobar o Beaglaoich mar don le congnamh Aodh bhridhe mac Cuirtin agus fós.* Paris: Guerin.

Boyle, Patrick (1901). *The Irish college in Paris from 1578 to 1901.* London: Art & Book Co.

Boyle, Patrick (1901a). Lord Iveagh and other Irish Officers, Students at the Collège des Grassins, in Paris, from 1684–1710. *Irish Ecclesiastical Record*, fourth series, 10, 385–94.

Boyle, Patrick (1905). The Abbé John Baptist Walsh D.D., Administrator of the Irish foundations in France from 1787–1815. *Irish Ecclesiastical Record*, fourth series, 18, 431–54.

Boyle, Patrick (1907). A plea for the Irish College in Paris. *Irish Ecclesiastical Record*, fourth series, 21, 285–299.

Boyle, Patrick (1908). The Abbé Charles Kearney, D.D. (1762–1824). His life and sufferings during the French Revolution. *Irish Ecclesiastical Record*, fourth series, 23, 454–466.

Brockliss, Lawrence W.B. and P. Ferté (1987). Irish Clerics in France in the Seventeenth and Eighteenth Centuries: A Statistical Study'. *Proceedings of the Royal Irish Academy*, 87C:9, 527–72.

Brockliss, Lawrence W.B. and P. Ferté (2004). A Prospography of Irish Clerics in the Universities of Paris and Toulouse. *Archivium Hibernicum*, 58, 7–166.

Burstin, Haim (2005). *Une révolution à l'oeuvre: le faubourg Saint-Marcel (1789–1794).* Seyssel: Éditions Champs Vallon.

Chambers, Liam (2006). Rivalry and reform in the Irish College, Paris, 1676–1775. In Thomas O'Connor and Mary Anne Lyons (eds.). *Irish communities in early modern Europe*, 103–29. Dublin: Four Courts Press.

Chambers, Liam (2009). Revolutionary and Refractory? The Irish Colleges in Paris and the French Revolution. *Journal of Irish and Scottish Studies*, 2, 1, forthcoming.

Cullen, L.M. (1994). The Irish Diaspora of the Seventeenth and Eighteenth Centuries. In Nicholas Canny (ed.). *Europeans on the Move: Studies on European Migration, 1500–1800*, 113–152. Oxford: Oxford University Press.

Daumet, G. (1910, 1912). Notices sur les établissements religieux Anglais, Écossais et Irlandais fondéees à Paris avant la revolution. *Mémoires de la société de l'histoire de Paris et de l'Ile-de-France,* 37, 1–184; 39, 1–224.

Donlevy, Andrew (1742). *The catechism, or Christian doctrine by way of question and answer.* Paris: Guerin.

Geoghegan, Vincent (1991). A Jacobite History: the Abbé MacGeoghegan's History of Ireland. *Eighteenth-century Ireland,* 6, 37–56.

[Henegan, David] (1759). *Irlande. In Le grand dictionnaire historique.* Paris: Les Libraires Associés.

Hibernicus Historicus [William Butler?] (1870). *The case and claims on the British Government of the Irish College at Paris under the treaties with France.* London: James Duffy.

Keogh, Dáire (1993). *The French Disease: the Catholic church and Irish radicalism, 1790–1800.* Dublin: Four Courts Press.

McBride, Ian (2001). Memory and national identity in modern Ireland. In Ian McBride (ed.). *History and memory in modern Ireland,* 1–42. Cambridge: Cambridge University Press.

Mac Cana Proinsias (2001). *Collège des Irlandais Paris & Irish Studies.* Dundalk: Dublin Institute for Advanced Studies.

McDonnell, J. (2002). From Bernini to Celtic Revival: A Tale of Two Irish Colleges in Paris. *Irish Arts Review,* 18, 165–175.

MacGeoghegan James (1758, 1762). *Histoire d'Irlande, ancienne et moderne.* Paris: Antoine Boudet.

O'Boyle James (1935). *The Irish colleges on the continent. Their origin and history.* Dublin: Browne & Nolan.

O'Brien, John (1768). *Focalóir gaoidhilge-sax-bhéarla or an Irish-English dictionary.* Paris: Nicolas-Francis Valleyre.

O'Connor, Priscilla (2006). *Irish Clerics in the University of Paris, 1570–1770.* Ph.D. diss., National University of Ireland, Maynooth.

O'Connor Thomas (1999). Towards the invention of the Irish Catholic natio: Thomas Messingham's Florilegium (1624). *Irish Theological Quarterly*, 64/2, 157–77.

O'Connor, Thomas (ed.) (2001). *The Irish in Europe, 1580–1815.* Dublin: Four Courts Press.

O'Connor, Thomas (2001a). Ireland and Europe, 1580–1815: some historiographical remarks. In Thomas O'Connor (ed.). *The Irish in Europe*, 9–26. Dublin: Four Courts Press.

O'Connor, Thomas and Mary Ann Lyons (eds.). (2003). *Irish migrants in Europe after Kinsale, 1602–1820.* Dublin: Four Courts Press.

O'Connor, Thomas and Mary Ann Lyons (eds.). (2006). *Irish communities in early modern Europe.* Dublin: Four Courts Press.

Purcell, Mary (1985). Richard Ferris, 1754–1828. *Journal of the Kerry Archaeological & Historical Society*, 18, 5–77.

Rapport, Michael (2000). *Nationality and Citizenship in Revolutionary France: The Treatment of Foreigners, 1789–1799.* Oxford: Oxford University Press.

Rapport, Michael (2002). A community apart? The closure of the Scots College in Paris during the French Revolution, 1789–1794. *The Innes Review*, 53, 1, 79–106.

Rothe, David (1620). *Brigidia thaumaturga.* Paris: Cramoisy.

Swords, Liam (ed.) (1978). *The Irish-French connection, 1578–1978.* Paris: The Irish College.

Swords, Liam (ed.) (1980). History of the Irish College, Paris, 1578–1800. Calendar of the Papers of the Irish College, Paris. *Archivium Hibernicum*, 35, 3–233

Swords, Liam (1985). *Soldiers, scholars, priests. A short history of the Irish College, Paris.* Paris: The Irish College.

Swords, Liam (1989). *The green cockade: the Irish in the French Revolution 1789–1815.* Dublin: Glendale Books.

Tuilier André (1994). *Histoire de L'Université de Paris et de La Sorbonne.* Paris: Nouvelle Librarie de France.

Walsh, T.J. (1973). *The Irish continental college movement: the colleges at Bordeaux, Toulouse and Lille.* Dublin: Golden Eagle Books.

Sephardi Jews – Cosmopolitans in the Atlantic World?*[1]

Susanne Lachenicht

In a late antique, medieval and early modern perspective, the notion of »cosmopolitan« was deployed to describe someone who stood outside existing cultures, observing them somewhat at a distance. Simultaneously, this cosmopolitan was able to move in and out of these cultures at will. Closely related to *ubi bene, ibi patria*-attitudes (»where things are good, there is one's homeland«), cosmopolitanism was not necessarily looked upon as an ideal, as cosmopolitans did not identify first and foremost as a citizen (or a subject) of one particular city or state. With Kant came a definition of cosmopolitanism that added notions and values such as the equality of all races, nations and religions. By the end of the eighteenth century, the transfer and exchange of knowledge, among members of the Republic of Letters and the Enlightenment and through increased commerce and trade, had led, in some areas, to the levelling down of religious and national identities and for a short period of time to concepts that represented cosmopolitanism as an ideal. In 1784, Rabaut Saint-Etienne, a French-reformed pastor at Nîmes and later member of the National Convention, claimed civil and equal rights not only for Protestants but also for all other

* I wish to thank Dr PJ Finglass for his suggestions while I was finishing this article.

1 »The Atlantic World« is an organizing concept for the historical study of the Atlantic Ocean rim. It emphasises inter-regional and international comparisons and draws attention to historical phenomena that transcended national borders. This article mainly focuses on the eastern Atlantic port cities. While it will show that the experience of the Sephardi diaspora in different Atlantic port cities might have been heterogenous, the Sephardi experience in the Atlantic world shares, nonetheless, many similar traits. It is fundamentally different from the Jewish diaspora in Central and Eastern Europe. As such, the Sephardi diaspora in the Atlantic world is one of the many topics that make evident that, with the European expansion in the Atlantic sphere, historical patterns, such as the accommodation of religious migrants, changed due to new needs in commerce and trade.

strangers to whatever religion they belonged (Rabaut Saint Etienne 1787). However, Rabaut Saint-Etienne's voice was a lonely voice. With the beginning of the wars of the French Revolution cosmopolitan ideas proved to be a short intermezzo. They soon vanished and were buried by nationalisms that would be the guidelines for European policy throughout the nineteenth century (Cohen 1997, 130–131; Kleingeld and Brown 2006).

The Sephardi diaspora has, as much as the Huguenot *Refuge*, been identified with notions of »cosmopolitanism« (Naphtali Hertz Wessel 1755, quoted in Schorsch 2002, 60), or, as Portuguese Jews in Amsterdam, as »reluctant cosmopolitans« (Swetschinski 2004). However, the term »reluctant cosmopolitan« could suggest that cosmopolitanism was an early modern ideal, which the Sephardim in Amsterdam should have met. However, this was not the case, as the following paragraphs will show.

Based on research that has been carried out by specialists of the Sephardi diaspora, this article will discuss, first, whether Portuguese Jews in Amsterdam, Bordeaux, London and the English colonies in North America were settled as separate nations or corporate bodies or whether they were supposed to integrate into the legal and cultural systems of the hosting societies. Second, I will ask whether the »Sephardi nation« was a concept lived by the majority of the Sephardim in diaspora or whether the Sephardi nation was a master narrative, created by the gate-keepers of this diaspora in order to forge and preserve a Portuguese Jewish identity outside the Iberian peninsula. Finally, I will investigate the extent to which members of the Sephardi diaspora displayed cosmopolitan attitudes or practices and how early modern governments and the Sephardi communities themselves reacted to those.

A Short Introduction to the Sephardi Diaspora

The Sephardi diaspora dates back to the expulsion of the Jews from the lands of the Catholic monarchs Isabella of Castile and Ferdinand of Aragon in 1492. Jews who had refused to convert to Catholicism were expelled. The great majority of Spain's Jews found refuge in North Africa, the Ottoman Empire, in Italy and, mainly, in Portugal. In 1497, King Manuel I of Portugal forcibly converted all Jews to Catholicism. As he feared the exodus of a great number of his *converso* subjects (also called *New*

Christians or *New Converts*), he chose not to enquire into the religious beliefs of the New Converts. Nonetheless, from the early sixteenth century onwards, Jewish merchants from Portugal started settling in Antwerp, Ancona, Ferrara, Venice and port cities of the Ottoman Empire. A network of Sephardi merchant communities was to establish itself in the Mediterranean and in the newly discovered Americas despite Manuel's attempts to prohibit emigration of his New Converts from Portugal. From 1536, with the establishment of the Portuguese Inquisition (it exerted its power from 1542), more New Converts left the Iberian peninsula in order to settle in Africa, Asia, Western Europe and the Americas. When in 1580 Spain and Portugal were unified under one crown, Portugal's New Christians were allowed to settle in Spain and the Spanish overseas colonies. However, with the influx of New Christians in Spain, suspicion as to their Catholic beliefs increased. Beginning in Portugal where the Inquisition persecuted more and more New Converts for their so-called crypto-Judaism, the entire Iberian world, including the colonies, was to develop an »anti-*converso* backlash« (Swetschinski 2004, 61). With the Dutch conquest of Brazil, the Spanish authorities suspected Jewish Portuguese merchants in the Dutch Republic and in the Spanish and Portuguese colonies of an anti-Spanish conspiracy that would have delivered Brazil to the Dutch. The international networks of the Sephardi diaspora had produced its first accusations of treason which was followed by an ever increasing Inquisition in Spain and the exodus of more Portuguese merchants from the Iberian Peninsula.

Accommodating Portuguese Jewish or Sephardi Communities

Sephardi Jews in Amsterdam and the Dutch overseas colonies

Article 13 of the 1579 Union of Utrecht had specified that the United Provinces of the Netherlands and within them local authorities had full sovereignty in religious matters as long as they respected freedom of conscience. Therefore, accommodating religious migrants, including non-Calvinist dissenters, was possible. However, at the Synod of Dort in 1618–19, the Dutch Reformed Church reaffirmed its hard-line Calvinism. Nonetheless, the United Provinces failed to become a Calvinist theocracy (Motley 1898, 159–65; Geyl 1961, 169–78). From some local authorities' understanding, some cities such as Amsterdam required immigrants. What the local authorities expected in return was the immigrants bringing some valuable skills, not only in the United Provinces but also in the Dutch overseas colonies such as New Amsterdam or Surinam (Huusen 2002, 26; Swetschinski 2004, 49–51).

In the bargaining between the authorities and the religious minority group that was to be accommodated not only utility but also the extent to which the minority group differed from the received Calvinist denomination played an important role. While Amsterdam admitted most of the Sephardi refugees, other towns in the Dutch Republic refused to admit New Converts or Jews at all (Huusen 2002, 39). In Amsterdam, the Sephardim faced more restrictions than Christian dissenters: Portuguese merchants, referred to as the Portuguese *natie*, were allowed to own property and purchase citizenship (*poortershap)* but they could not pass it on to their children or acquire it by marriage. They were excluded from some of the guilds, yet special allowances were made for the sugar refiners in 1655 and tobacconists in 1668. Further exceptions were made for physicians, surgeons, apothecaries and booksellers (Huusen 2002, 34–6; Swetschinski 2004, 10, 20–2, 165; Catterall 2007, 74–80).

Essentially not the will to practice religious tolerance but to strengthen the economic and political power of the young United Provinces dictated the acceptance of other nations of outsider groups within the Republic (Frijhoff 2002, 27–52; Israel 1998, 372, 655, 676, 1033; Kaplan 2002, 1; Po-Chia Hsia 2002, 2–3). It is important to state that the provinces and cities who admitted religious dissenters did not expect integration or assimilation of these groups but, instead, settled them as separate groups or as separate nations. *Naçao* (nation), as Daniel M. Swetschinski has put it, »suggests both distinctiveness from society at large and an identity of interest and purpose within the group« (Swetschinski 2004, 166).

With the first arrival of Portuguese New Christians in Amsterdam in the early 1590s, the city fathers presumed that they were Christians indeed. They did not enquire into the immigrants' religious practices. By the last years of the sixteenth and the early seventeenth century, however, it had become obvious that most of these New Christians had (re-)converted to Judaism. During the second decade of the seventeenth century, Amsterdam's city fathers allowed the Portuguese Jewish community to erect a synagogue even if the building belonged to one of Amsterdam's senators. Still, officially, Jews were not allowed to practice their faith in public (Kaplan 2002, 2).

With Amsterdam's Sephardi Jews officially professing Judaism came the loss of their status as (former) subjects of the Kings of Portugal or Spain, a status which they had enjoyed as New Christians. In Amsterdam, the Portuguese nation became both a religious association and a foreign merchant colony (Swetschinski 2004, 185).

According to early modern models in the accommodation of stranger communities or foreign nations, during the 1620s Amsterdam's Portuguese Jews had to establish their own community administration, mainly for means of poor relief. Also, it had to represent the community in judicial affairs that involved other nations within Amsterdam. Some researchers have argued that Amsterdam's Portuguese nation formed a corporation or that Amsterdam's city fathers had explicitly settled the Portuguese nation as a corporate body with specific legal connotations (Catterall 2007, 50–80). Huusen and Swetschinski find that Amsterdam's city fathers, who had no experience with accommodating Jewish communities prior to the 1590s, reduced the autonomy of Amsterdam's Jewish communities as they interfered with internal heritage and marital affairs and tried to impose civil marriage on Jewish couples. Also, Amsterdam's Jews paid municipal and state taxes to the City of Amsterdam (and the United Provinces) individually, not *in solidum* or collectively through the congregation which would have been the case in many Central and Eastern European towns and cities. Hence Amsterdam's city fathers referred to the Portuguese merchants as a nation (*natie*) but did not clearly define their legal status in the city. In some matters, Amsterdam attempted to legally integrate the Portuguese nation into the dominant society (Huusen, 2002, 34–5, 39; Swetschinski 2004, 15–19, 197).

In Dutch Brazil, with the Truce of 1641 between the Netherlands and Portugal, Sephardi Jews were granted the same privileges their brethren enjoyed in the United Provinces. They were excluded only from a few professions and from holding magistracies and civic offices. In Dutch Brazil, the Sephardim came as close to legal and economic equality with Christians as they were ever to attain in the Western world before the French Revolution (Israel 2002, 367—383–4, 511). The Catholic resurrection in Dutch Brazil in 1645 almost destroyed Sephardi communities in Recife, Mauricia, Paraiba and Itamaraca. Here, the Sephardi experience came to an end in 1654 when the Dutch garrison of Recife had to surrender to Portuguese assaults (Israel 2002, 368, 382).

Bordeaux

When after the establishment of the Inquisition in Portugal in 1536 many so-called New Christian families fled the Iberian Peninsula, some of them settled north the Pyrenees in the south-west of France; mainly in Bordeaux, Toulouse, Saint-Jean-de-Luz, Peyrehorade, Biarritz and Bayonne. They settled as New Converts or *conversos*, so as officially Catholicism professing merchants. In 1550, the French king Henry II passed a decree naturalizing these *Portuguese merchants*, promising them royal protection. Furthermore, he allowed them freedom of trade. This decree was reconfirmed in 1574 (and again in 1656 and 1723), two years after another religious minority in France, the French Calvinists had been murdered in thousands during the night of St Bartholomew. The 1574 decree was an ordinance indicating that no maltreatment of these Portuguese merchants would be tolerated and, furthermore, that no enquiry would be made into their religious practices. This guarantee already indicates some knowledge, on the part of the crown, of the origins of these Portuguese merchants and the existence among them of elements that did not exhibit Catholic Christian behaviour. When in 1580 Spain and Portugal were unified under one crown, more New Christians arrived in the South of France.[2] The economic activity of the *marchands portugais* seems to have been especially valuable for the crown and explains the relatively tolerant attitude toward this group. The *parlement* of Bordeaux did not agree with the royal decrees. It registered the royal decrees of 1550 and 1574 only in 1580. From then onwards, it officially allowed Portuguese merchants into the city and continued to privilege Portuguese merchants even when, in 1602, Henry IV ordered the expulsion of the Portuguese from Bayonne. Further royal attempts towards the expulsion of the Portuguese merchants were met by one and the same procedure: the *parlement* of Bordeaux refused to register the royal decree (Malino 1978, 2–26; Israel 1985, 51–2; Benbassa 1999, 50–2).

The Edict of Fontainebleau of 1685 and the flight of some 150,000 to 200,000 French Protestants from France had made the co-existence of

2 It is estimated in a 1633 report that there were forty Jewish families in Bordeaux, sixty in Bayonne, eighty at Labastide-Clairence, forty at Peyrehorade, ten at Dax, twenty at Rouen, and twelve in Paris. This settlement increased further during the contreband trade that followed the trade embargo on Holland that Spain imposed from 1621 to 1647.

different religious denominations or nations rather unlikely. The design of Louis XIV to establish religious orthodoxy throughout his kingdom, which included the expulsion of all Jews, ran counter the interests of the port city of Bordeaux expressed by Louis' intendant M. de Bezons. Bordeaux feared the city's economic downturn if some of their most important merchants, the Portuguese *conversos*, were to leave town. From 1693, the city of Bordeaux granted the Sephardi community, the *nation portugaise*, the right to self-organisation structures. It was to establish a *Société de Bienfaisance*, the *Sedaca*, in order to organise the poor relief of the Sephardi community, to erect and maintain *kosher* meat shops, ritual bath houses and religious schools. Furthermore, the *Sedaca* took control of the Sephardi community life in all social matters and levied taxes to maintain the institutions of the community (Malino 1978, 9–10).

While the city of Bordeaux's interest in keeping its Portuguese merchants increased, the crown, in 1722, was no longer willing to accept Bordeaux's Portuguese merchants as New Christians but addressed them now as Jews. They were to be subject to the same taxes and laws as Ashkenazi communities in Metz and Lorraine. Again, Bordeaux's intendant feared for the prosperity of the city. Her petitions to Louis XV must have been convincing. In 1723, Bordeaux's Sephardi community received royal Letter Patents which allowed them privileges similar to the ones they had enjoyed since the 1550s. Additionally, they were now officially recognised as Jews. Medieval Jews legislation was not to be introduced in Bordeaux. From 1723, the legal status of the Sephardim there was similar to the one their brethren had enjoyed in Amsterdam from the early 1600s: they were restricted to some commercial activities, were not to become members of the guilds, could not become members of the Chamber of Commerce and could not exert municipal functions within the Christian municipality (Malino 1978, 6–7, 19).

Despite temporary opposition from Bordeaux's merchants, from the eighteenth century onward the Sephardi Jews of Bordeaux formed the Jewish nation of Bordeaux, a *res publica* responsible for its members. In 1760, the French king approved the *Règlement de la nation des Juifs Portugais.* The Jewish Portuguese Nation appointed an official agent in Paris, Jacob Rodrigues-Pereira (1715–1780), to act as intermediary between them and the crown. The *règlement* allowed them to elect an assembly to determine who was to be part of this nation. With the *règlement*, it exerted power over the Sephardi community by royal authorisation. From 1763, the Sephardim were not hindered from professing Judaism. Indeed, they were often naturalised subjects enjoying virtually all rights, including the right to purchase land and the freedom to choose their residential neighbourhood without having to wear a distinctive badge (Benbassa 1999, 50–2).

England and the English Colonies

In 1290, King Edward I issued a decree which would lead to the general expulsion of the Jews from England. However, after the edict of the expulsion of the Jews from Spain (1492), Sephardi Jews had settled, albeit in small numbers, in England, particularly in London. Despite the statute *De haeretico comburendo* which made it a capital crime in England for any baptised Christian to practise Judaism, *conversos* were important in London in trade and commerce. As in Bordeaux, some of the Sephardim, officially recognised as New Christians, were denizened in England. A short intermezzo put the existence of London's Jewish community in jeopardy. In 1609 King James I expelled most of the Portuguese Jews from England. Twenty-six years later, newly arriving Portuguese Jews or New Christians were allowed to re-settle. In 1641, the Long Parliament repealed the *Act Concerning the Burning of Heretics* (Samuel 2006, 131).

During the Cromwellian era, England faced an amalgamation of Jewish and Christian millenerial ideas of a union of Jews and Puritans. Interpretations of biblical prophecies indicated that Jews and Christians would be united when the Messiah appeared or reappeared. Even though only a small number of people shared these ideas in England, they deeply influenced Cromwell and his policy towards Jews. Puritan theologians proclaimed that England was the New Israel. Cromwell and his entourage insisted that only the English Protestants were pure enough of spirit to make the Jews realise that Christianity was the fulfilment of Judaism (Weiner 1994, 58–63; Samuel 1988–1990).

With Cromwell going to war against Spain, Spanish merchants in England were likely to be dispossessed of their property. Emerging openly as Jews became, from 1655 onwards, *a better bet* in order to survive as a merchant community and as religious refugees in Cromwellian London. Menasseh Ben Israel's attempts to instigate the formal readmission of Jews into England failed at the Whitehall Conference in 1655. However, in 1664 Sephardi Jews were officially allowed to practice Judaism as long as they did so peaceably, without scandal to the government, the Anglican Church or English society. The community's first synagogue had been erected in 1657 (Israel 1985, 158–60; Samuel 176, 186–8; Katz 1994; Samuel 2006, 179, 186–8).

Contrary to Bordeaux's merchants and Amsterdam's city fathers, London merchants opposed the re-settlement of the Jews in London fearing competition in the Atlantic trade. For Cromwell, the Sephardim of London furnished valuable military expertise for his campaign against Spain in the West Indies. During the Cromwellian era, London's Sephardim were much more »court Jews« than »port Jews« as the city itself was not interested in Sephardi settlement. William III, again, whose military campaigns in the British Isles and in Europe relied heavily on Sephardi army contractors such as the Machado and Pereira company, had to push through pro-Sephardi declarations against the interest of London's merchant elite and local interests in the West Indies (Endelman 1979, 21; Fortune 1984, 7, 11–12; Israel 1985, 128–32; Cesarini 2002, 111, 117–8, Israel 2002, 522–3).

With the end of the Interregnum and the restoration of the Stuarts in 1660, English philo-semitic politics came to an end. Some medieval laws governed the Sephardi community in London (Cesarini 2002, 117), a situation which differed fundamentally from that of Bordeaux or Amsterdam. However, before 1689 most of London's Jews were endenizened. Attempts to make Parliament enact general naturalisation, as was the case in 1753, failed. Nonetheless, during the eighteenth century, the Jewish community of London grew rapidly. Many New Christians from Portugal arrived in England, as England was becoming Portugal's largest trading partner. By 1753 there were some 2,000 Sephardi Jews and some 4,000 Ashkenazi Jews in London. Jews mostly worked as merchants, engravers, confectioners, tailors, silk throwers, translators and language teachers (Spanish and Portuguese), as stock, diamond and pearl brokers, some were insurance brokers. Jews were not allowed to work as solicitors or barristers, but as public notaries. Medicine, a respected profession of the Jews in Spain and Portugal, was closed to them in England, as they were not admitted to the universities (Yogev 1978). This was also true for all other non-Anglicans in eighteenth century England.

In the overseas colonies, the English government was more successful in granting non-Christian communities considerable corporative rights. In Surinam, between 1652 and 1667 (up to the end of English rule there), Sephardi Jews enjoyed freedom of religion and were allowed to practice their Jewish faith in public. Their privileges included the erection of synagogues, political autonomy, the right to defend themselves (with their own militia) and the right to take land. The late Stuarts continued Cromwell's policies towards Sephardi Jewish settlements, refusing to cut back privileges granted in the 1650s to Sephardi communities on Barbados and Jamaica (Fortune 1984, 33–4, 44). On Jamaica, Sephardi Jewish communities enjoyed the same privileges as in Surinam; English colonisers hoped thereby to improve commerce and establish more sugar refineries. In the 1660s many Jews acquired denization, some of them were naturalised. In New York, Jews were permitted religious freedom under English rule (Goodfriend 1992, 84). Other English colonies, such as Virginia, Maryland and the Carolinas, were not willing to accommodate Sephardi Jews on these terms; but in 1740 the British government granted Sephardi Jews general naturalisation in its overseas colonies (Kerem 2001, 286–7, 291–2).

Judaism, »Nationalism« and Integration Patterns

Amsterdam

In Amsterdam, New Christians arriving in the city from the 1590s onwards started professing Judaism, which the city fathers did not oppose. By 1610, Amsterdam had three distinct Jewish congregations which unified in 1639 and became the Kahal Kados de Talmud Tora (Swetschinski 2004, 4, 167, 174).

In addition to city taxes, the *Mahamad* (the governance of the Kahal Kados de Talmud Tora which consisted of seven elders, six *parnassim* (members of the community) and one *gabai* (treasurer)) levied taxes for the community's own purposes such as the maintenance of synagogues, schools, ritual bath houses, for *kosher* meat and social welfare. The *Mahamad* oversaw its members' behaviour in domains of charity, worship (including Sabbath observance) and education. It also exerted social control over individuals and families with regard to gambling, monogamy, ethnic endogamy, prostitution and illegitimate offspring. Transgressive members could be threatened with fines and excommunication. In order to preserve the community as an intact separate nation, the Talmud Tora School was to educate boys in Hebrew, reading the Torah and the Prophets, translating from Hebrew into Spanish and studying Talmud and Jewish law. The extent to which families benefitted from these institutions is hard to determine. Integration or acculturation took place as Dutch tutors were employed to instruct children in Dutch and Dutch handwriting: speaking Dutch was necessary for professions such as apothecaries, merchants and salesmen, physicians and booksellers. Studying medicine and law at Dutch universities also required Jews to step outside their community. Nonetheless, Amsterdam's Sephardi community preserved Portuguese as their main everyday language. Male community members were supposed to learn Hebrew to enable them to participate in Jewish worship (Bodian 1999, 63–8; Israel 2002, 185; Swetschinski 2004, 199–210–1, 213, 216–7, 226–7, 278–80, 284). As Daniel M. Swetschinski has put it: »In their cultural as well as their religious life, of course, these immigrants remained a group apart. They wanted it that way; and the people among them whom they lived did not seem to be bothered by their self-sufficiency« (Swetschinski 2004, 5).

The Portuguese nation in Amsterdam referred to itself either as the *naçao ebrea* or as the *naçao portuguesa*, highlighting their ethnic and their religious distinctness. The term *naçao portuguesa* prevailed in the first decades following their establishment in Amsterdam: up to the early seventeenth century, the Portuguese nation was not entitled to profess Judaism in public. From the 1600s onwards, with the establishment of a Portuguese nation officially professing Judaism, Amsterdam began to refer to the Portuguese nation as a religious association as well.

In Dutch Brazil, the Truce of 1641 led to the New Converts not only returning to the faith of their ancestors but to proselytizing other New Christians and crypto-Jews. As much as in Amsterdam and later in the century in Bordeaux, a Sephardi community emerged officially practising Judaism. The Catholic resurrection in Dutch Brazil in 1645 almost destroyed Sephardi communities in Recife, Mauricia, Paraiba and Itamaraca (Israel 2002, 368).

Amsterdam's Portuguese nation attempted to remain distinct from Dutch society and Calvinists. It also refused to accept Ashkenazi Jews (or Sephardim who had married an Ashkenazi Jew) into its communities, and assigned to black and mulatto Jews an inferior status within the Sephardi society. The latter were buried in a separate section of the Sephardi community's cemetery. Social, ethnic and religious endogamy among Amsterdam's Portuguese nation was crucial to safeguard group and family identity. This was particularly true of the Portuguese *élite* of Amsterdam (Swetschinski 2004, 188–9, 194–5, 251; Schorsch 2002; Schorsch 2004).

From the early 1600s the Portuguese enclave in Amsterdam was as much defined by its ethnic origins as by its Jewish religion. Its »nationalism« was of ethnic and of religious origin. While Amsterdam's city fathers had not clearly defined the legal status of the Portuguese *natie*, the Portuguese nation defined itself both as a foreign *kerck* (church) and a foreign colony, with its own administration, jurisdiction and law, which attempted to remain distinct from Dutch society (Bodian 1999, 85–95). This is a pattern commonly found among religious refugees such as French Huguenots, whose character as a »nation abroad« was formed by both their having been persecuted for their faith at home and having been identified as of a distinct »nation« in diaspora (Lachenicht 2007 and 2009; Van Ruymbeke 2009).

As much as other early modern diasporas, the Sephardi nation of Amsterdam entertained bonds with other Portuguese Jewish communities in the Atlantic world, through networks that guaranteed commerce and trade, relief for New Converts in or from the Iberian peninsula in need of help and relief, for marriage and the orthodoxy of their religious beliefs. This was to strengthen the religious and ethnic distinctness of the Sephardi Jewish nation in diaspora and transcended state borders (Swetschinski 2004, 203). For the northern European Sephardi diaspora Amsterdam was to become the »mother community« (Bodian 1999, 141).

However, as for many other religious diasporas in the early modern period, acculturation and integration into the hosting society were on their way. From the mid-seventeenth century onwards, more and more members of Amsterdam's Portuguese nation adopted elements of Dutch culture and blended them into their Iberian-Jewish culture. (Swetschinski 2004, 285–286, 312, 322–323). From the late seventeenth century, some members of Amsterdam's Portuguese Jewish intellectual elites became interested in ideas of the Republic of Letters and the Enlightenment and engaged in erudite discourse (Bodian 1999, 116). This has often been described as cosmopolitan attitudes (Bodian 1999, 116) which, as much as with the Huguenots (Lachenicht 2007), were counterbalanced by conservative and »nationalist« attitudes of the Sephardi nation. If we understand pre-Kantian cosmopolitanism as switching between two or more cultures, as ambivalent or heterodox attitudes and practices, the *Mahamad* did not accept cosmopolitanism (Bodian 1999, 110–25).

Furthermore, some Portuguese New Converts who arrived in Amsterdam in the 1600s did not integrate into the existing Jewish congregations. Being technically members of the *naçao Portuguesa* of Amsterdam, they refused to become members of the Jewish communities in town (Bodian 1999, 112–113; Israel 2002, 197; Swetschinski 2004, 166–167, 175, 185). The *Mahamad* attempted to integrate these »ambivalent and heterodox« (Bodian 1999, 110), which meant that they were to be put under the government of the *parnassim* in jurisdictional, social and cultural matters. Sephardi Jews who attempted to live outside the community were denied the right of burial or suffered anathema/ban (*herem*) (Bodian 1999, 113–114). Equally problematic for the Jewish community and Portuguese Jewish group identity were returnees, *New Christians* having arrived in Amsterdam or other places of the Sephardi diaspora who returned to the Iberian peninsula where they re-converted from Judaism to Catholicism (Graizbord 2003; Muchnik 2002; Studemund-Halévy 2005). This phenomenon is not only known in the Sephardi context but also for other so-called religious refugees such as French Calvinists or Huguenots (Lachenicht 2010, chapter 4).

In the long run, acculturation changed the outlook of the Sephardi nation in Amsterdam indeed. By the end of the eighteenth century, the *Mahamad* could no longer prevent members from integrating into Christian and Dutch society. With the French Revolution and the conquest of the Netherlands came the end of self-government of distinct religious and ethnic communities (Bodian 1999, 156–61).

Bordeaux

Immediately after their arrival in the mid-1500s, the Sephardim of Bordeaux had behaved like Christians and had practiced intermarriage with the Catholic population. But between 1690 and 1700, many Sephardi Jews ceased to have their children baptised. Around 1711 many of their marriages were no longer blessed by the Catholic Church, and they increasingly practiced social endogamy. Before the later seventeenth century it had seemed that both crypto-Jews among France's New Christians and the pro-Catholic party among that same group had an equal influence on Christian or crypto-Jewish attitudes among the Sephardi communities. From the late seventeenth century onwards there emerged a new community of Sephardim officially practising Judaism in Bordeaux and other cities in south-west France. They had their own synagogues, schools, ritual baths and communal institutions; their language was Spanish or Portuguese. Still in the eighteenth century the Sephardi culture blended with elements of French culture, as French was taught in the Bordeaux Jews' schools. Yet few of them converted to Christianity throughout the eighteenth century (Malino 1978, 5, 11, 20; Israel 2002, 245, 255–63).

It has often been asked why Bordeaux's New Converts, who seemed to have blended into Christian society by the late seventeenth century, became a distinct Jewish community later. With Don Pedro of Portugal's decision to ban alls New Converts from his kingdom, at least those whom the Inquisition had condemned for crypto-Judaism, a new wave of New Converts arrived in Bordeaux. They gave the community of New Converts a more distinct Sephardi Jewish feature. Furthermore, seeking corporate status as a Jewish community in Bordeaux was looked upon as giving the Sephardim more secure a legal basis in the city of Bordeaux. Being established as a corporation not only provided the Sephardim of Bordeaux but also other outsider groups with a secure framework of privileges necessary to maintain Atlantic trade and commerce, their religious beliefs and their languages (Molino 1978, 11–13).

On the eve of the French Revolution of 1789, despite the edict of expulsion of 1394, about 40,000 Jews lived in France, forming a group of *nations* within the French state, distinct from French Christian subjects and each other. The Portuguese Jewish community of Bordeaux refused to accept Jewish immigrants from Avignon, considering the Jews of the east of France to be »foreigners« and backward. Nor did Bordeaux's Sephardim admit Ashkenazi Jews to their *nation* (Molino 1978, 20).

With the royal edict of November 1787 granting civil status to Calvinists the situation of the Jewish minorities in France came under re-consideration. The Sephardim of Bordeaux rejected civil equality, and pleaded for the continuation and confirmation of the royal letter patents granted between 1550 and 1776. But their pleas were ignored, and in 1791, with the first Constitution of the French Revolution, all Jews of France became citizens on condition that they renounced their communal status.

London

From the 1650s Sephardi Jews were safer from persecution in London if they openly converted from *New Converts* of the Portuguese or Spanish nation to Judaism. Hence in London Jewish life and a Jewish community came to be established from the mid-seventeenth century. Following the Amsterdam model, London's Sephardi Jews established their own community led by elders from the Amsterdam community. As in Amsterdam and Bordeaux, the *parnassim* attempted to exert tight control over the religious and social behaviour of London's Portuguese Jews (Samuel 2006, 197–198).

Forming one Portuguese Jewish nation in London proved to be more difficult than in Amsterdam. Many newly arriving *conversos* were reluctant to undergo circumcision and obey the government of the *hamam*. After 1664, many of London's *New Jews* (Kaplan 1994) continued habits they had had as *New Christians* and led a fuzzy existence between Christian and Jewish rituals and lifestyles.

From the early eighteenth century wealthy Portuguese Jews imitated English life-style through dress, the cutting of beards or the acquisition of country-houses. Synagogue attendance decreased, intermarriage increased. By the mid-eighteenth century, it appears that the upper and upper middle class ranks of the Portuguese Jewish nation of London had become anglicised: their Portuguese Jewish identity coexisted with an English identity. The Jewish *petite bourgeoisie* despised this hybridity and retained social endogamy, Jewish rituals and brotherhoods up to at least the early nineteenth century (Endelman 1979, 4, 122, 125–6, 132–3, 135–8; Kaplan 1992, 234; Goldish 1994, 248–249; Melammed 2004, 97–103).

Sephardi Communities and Cosmopolitanism/Internationalism

While port cities such as Bordeaux or London took profit of the Portuguese merchants' international networks (Dubin 2002, 52; Schorsch 2002, 59), states such as France, the United Provinces, England and the Portuguese merchants' homelands Spain and Portugal suspected the Sephardim of treason, particularly during times of war between the states that served as these Portuguese merchants' base for trade and commerce within the

Old and with the New World. Amsterdam's Sephardim maintained close ties with New Converts in the Iberian Peninsula and sometimes even with the Spanish Court (Israel 2002, 198–208), some of them as spies in its service. This rendered Sephardi communities equivocal. Sephardi Jewish internationalism also meant that former *conversos* having (re-)converted to Judaism returned to Spain for commercial or diplomatic purposes, where they briefly established themselves in Spain's port cities or at the royal court. Provided with special licenses, these Sephardim were Jews who openly professed Judaism. As they openly refused Christian baptism, they distinguished themselves from crypto-Jews and New Converts. While the Inquisition feared that these real Jews would re-convert the *conversos* to Judaism (Muchnik 2005), Amsterdam's, Bordeaux's or London's city fathers were not entirely sure about these »internationalists« loyalism towards the national interests of the hosting country either. Suspicion also arose on Barbados and Jamaica where Sephardi Jews enjoyed considerable privileges from the 1650s. As most of them were of Portuguese or Dutch descent, English settlers and planters regarded them as collaborationists of the Dutch, against English economic and military interests in the Caribbean (Fortune 1984; Israel 2002, 522–524).

That some Portuguese Jews used different names (*aliases*), raised suspicion as well. Sephardi merchants operated across the entire Atlantic world. They took on different names by which they could be identified by their ethnically diverse trading partners. This was the case with Amsterdam's Ishac da Costa alias Jacques Gedellian, nicknamed the »devil of Vloyenburgh«, his associate Antonio Sanches de Pas alias Semuel Aboab or Jacob Delmont alias Jacob del Sotto alias Cornelis Cox Dircksz. The *alias* more often than not reflected the route of migration the family had taken or the diverse family branches and trading partners in the Mediterranean and/or Atlantic world (Swetschinski 2004, 228, 252–253, 280).

Moving between two or even more than two worlds was essential for many members of the Portuguese Jewish diaspora, such as merchants, physicians, apothecaries, diplomats, brokers and others. These international »players« often not only used different names but changed costume when travelling outside their home communities. While some states and cities insisted on special Jewish dress code, in order to identify and treat Jews as Jews, Amsterdam allowed its Portuguese Jews to dress in Christian garments. In many other contexts Jews who wore Christian garment were suspected of mimicry or attempting to conceal their true religion. In Spain and Portugal they were thus suspected of being potential Judaizers in disguise (Muchnik 2005, 128–129).

What has often been identified as the Sephardi Jews' cosmopolitanism was – for some professions at least – a necessary variety of distinct attitudes which allowed members of the Sephardi diaspora to survive economically and socially. To complicate things further, many members of the Sephardi diaspora displayed a hybridity of religious if not ethnic identities, due to the *converso* experience. The ethnic and religious Portuguese Jewish nation as it emerged in diaspora was of hybrid nature (Melammed 2004, 15–16, 24).

Concluding Remarks

Confessional barriers hindered expansion and profit. As the example of the Sephardim makes clear, in the Atlantic world some governments developed patrimonial interest in migrant groups. This is not only true for the Dutch Republic and its overseas colonies where diverse corporate groups such as the Sephardim, Ashkenazim or Scottish Presbyterians were accommodated, as has often been emphasised, but it is also true for the Sephardim in Bordeaux, London and some of the English Colonies. The governments offered protection and, after a time, religious tolerance. The Sephardi experience in Amsterdam, Bordeaux, London, Surinam, Jamaica and Barbados is far from homogenous. Nonetheless, it is a striking common feature that the New Converts developed, after a few decades, into a separate Portuguese Jewish nation with self-organisation structures. They gained corporate rights which enabled them to prosper as the Portuguese-Jewish nation across borders and states.

Compared to Eastern European Jews and Central European »Court Jews«, Sephardi Jews enjoyed improved legal status in most Atlantic port cities. Benefitting from what Lois Dubin terms »civil inclusion«, Port Jews lived in »corporate societies based on privileges« (Dubin 1999; Sorkin 2002, 37). In most Atlantic port cities, Sephardi Jews were not subject to special Jewry laws, as typical of Central and Eastern Europe, but were admitted as a foreign merchant corporation that later became a religious association as well. They thus established themselves as a separate ethnic and religious nation which – in the French and English cases – through denization and individual naturalisation could gain access to some of the privileges of the dominant society. In Amsterdam, limited legal inclusion was possible through the *poortershap* (Sorkin 2002, 37–8).

Not only the Spanish Inquisition and the Holy See attempted to ban cosmopolitan or internationalist practices and sought to force Jews to wear distinctive costume and use Jewish names (Muchnik 2005, 136). Also the Jewish communities in diaspora were eager to unite the Portuguese of the Jewish nation, to prohibit heterodox or ambivalent attitudes and identities, and to create and safeguard a diaspora identity that could protect Sephardi Jews from persecution in exile.

To what extent the majority of the Sephardim in Amsterdam, Bordeaux, London and the colonies adhered to and shared the exclusiveness of the Portuguese Jewish nation in diaspora is hard to determine. There is evidence that processes of acculturation were already on their way with the first arrival of New Converts in the eastern Atlantic port cities in the late sixteenth century, despite the return to Judaism and separate Jewish communities after a few generations. The master narrative of the Portuguese Jewish nation might have been appealing in some economic, social, political or cultural contexts, but could hinder survival and some individuals' or families' prosperity in others. Hosting societies and Portuguese Jewish communities might have been inclined to ban cosmopolitan attitudes and practices, ambivalence and heterodoxy, and might have wished to establish clearly separate nations. In the Atlantic world, however, where commerce and trade depended on mobility and exchange, acculturation and hybridity were the norm, regardless of the attitudes of the parties involved.

Works cited

Benbassa, Esther (2001). *The Jews of France. A History from Antiquity to the Present.* Princeton/NJ: Princeton University Press.

Bodian, Miriam (1999). *Hebrews of the Portuguese Nation. Conversos and Community in Early Modern Amsterdam.* Bloomington: Indiana University Press.

Catterall, Douglas (2007). Scots and Portuguese Migrants in the United Provinces (16th–17th centuries). In Susanne Lachenicht (ed.). *Religious Refugees in Europe, Asia and North America (6th–21st century)*, 53–80. Hamburg: LIT.

Cesarini, David (2002). Port Jews: Concepts, Cases and Questions. In David Cesarini (ed.). *Port Jews. Jewish Communities in Cosmopolitan Maritime Trading Centres, 1550–1950*, 1–11. London, Portland/OR: Frank Cass.

Cesarini, David (2002). The Forgotten Port Jews of London. In David Cesarini (ed.). *Port Jews. Jewish Communities in Cosmopolitan Maritime Trading Centres, 1550–1950*, 111–124. London, Portland/OR: Frank Cass.

Cohen, Robin (1997). *Global Diasporas: An Introduction.* Seattle: Routledge.

Dubin, Lois (1999). *The Port Jews of Habsburg Trieste.* Stanford: Stanford University Press.

Dubin, Lois (2002). Researching Port Jews and Port Jewries: Trieste and Beyond. In David Cesarini (ed.). *Port Jews. Jewish Communities in Cosmopolitan Maritime Trading Centres, 1550–1950*, 47–58. London, Portland/OR: Frank Cass.

Endelman, Todd M. (1979). *The Jews of Georgian England, 1714–1830. Tradition and Change in a Liberal Society.* Philadelphia: The Jewish Publication Society of America.

Forster, Marc R. (2005). Review of Kaspar von Greyerz, Manfred Jakubowski-Tiessen, Thomas Kaufmann and Hartmut Lehmann (eds.). *Interkonfessionalität – Transkonfessionalität – binnenkonfessionelle Pluralität: Neue Forschungen zur Konfessionalisierungsthese.* https://www.h-net.org/reviews/showpdf.php?id=10561. Accessed 6 June 2009.

Fortune, Stephen A. (1984). *Merchants and Jews: The Struggle for British West Indian Commerce, 1650–1750.* Gainesville/FL: University Press of Florida.

Frijhoff, Willem (2002). Religious Toleration in the United Provinces: from »case« to »model«. In Ronnie Po-chia Hsia and Henk van Nierop (eds.). *Calvinism and Religious Toleration in the Dutch Golden Age*, 27–52. Cambridge: Cambridge University Press.

Geyl, Pieter (1961). *The Netherlands in the Seventeenth Century.* 2 vols. London, New York: Barnes and Noble.

Goldish, Matt (1994). Jews, Christians, and Conversos: Rabbi Solomon Aailion's Struggles in the Portuguese Community of London. *Journal of Jewish Studies* 45, 227–257.

Goodfriend, Joyce D. (1992). *Before the melting pot: society and culture in colonial New York City, 1664–1730.* Princeton: Princeton University Press.

Graizbord, David (2003). *Souls in Dispute. Converso Identities in Iberia and the Jewish Diaspora, 1580–1700.* Philadelphia: W.W. Norton and Company.

Huusen, Arend H. (2002). The Legal Position of the Jews in the Dutch Republic, 1590–1796. In Jonathan I. Israel and Reinier Salverda (eds.). *Dutch Jewry. Its History and Secular Cultures (1500–2000)*, 25–41. Leiden, Boston, Cologne: Brill.

Israel, Jonathan I, (1985). *European Jewry in the Age of Mercantilism, 1550–1750.* Oxford: Clarendon Press.

Israel, Jonathan I. (1998). *The Dutch Republic: Its Rise, Greatness and Fall, 1477–1806.* Oxford, New York: Oxford University Press.

Israel, Jonathan I. (2002). *Diasporas within a Diaspora. Jews, Crypto-Jews and the World Maritime Empires (1540–1740).* Leiden, Boston, Cologne: Brill.

Kaplan, Benjamin (2002,1). »Dutch« religious tolerance: celebration and revision. In Ronnie Po-chia Hsia and Henk van Nierop (eds.). *Calvinism and Religious Toleration in the Dutch Golden Age*, 8–52. Cambridge: Cambridge University Press.

Kaplan, Benjamin (2002,2). Fictions of Privacy: House Chapels and the Spatial Accommodation of Religious Dissent in Early Modern Europe. *American Historical Review*, 107, 1031–1064.

Kaplan, Yosef (1992). The Jewish Profile of the Spanish-Portuguese Community of London. *Judaism*, 41, 229–240.

Kaplan, Yosef (1994). Wayward New Christians and Stubborn New Jews: The Shaping of Jewish Identity. *Jewish History*, 8, 27–41.

Katz, David S. (1994). *The Jews in the History of England.* Oxford: Oxford University Press.

Kerem, Yitzchak (2001). Sephardic Settlement in the British Colonies of the Americas in the 17th and 18th centuries. In Randolph Vigne and Charles Littleton (eds.). *From Strangers to Citizens. The Integration of Immigrant Communities in Britain, Ireland and Colonial America, 1550–1750*, 285–295. Brighton, Portland: Sussex Academic Press.

Kleingeld, Pauline and Eric Brown. Cosmopolitanism. For *Stanford Encyclopedia of Philosophy*, http://plato.stanford.edu, 2006 (revised and updated version of 2002 entry). Accessed 4 April 2009.

Kushner, Tony (2002). A Tale of Two Port Jewish Communities: Southampton and Portsmouth Compared. In David Cesarini (ed.). *Port Jews. Jewish Communities in Cosmopolitan Maritime Trading Centres, 1550–1950*, 87–110. London, Portland/OR: Frank Cass.

Lachenicht, Susanne (2007). Huguenot Immigrants and the Formation of National Identities. *The Historical Journal*, 50/2, 309–331.

Lachenicht, Susanne (2009). Culture Clash and Hubris. The History and Historiography of the Huguenots in Germany and the Atlantic World. In: Gesa Mackenthun and Sünne Juterczenka (eds.). *The fuzzy logic of encounter. New perspectives on cultural contact*, 75–96. Münster, New York, Munich, Berlin: Waxmann.

Lachenicht, Susanne (forthcoming 2010). *Hugenotten in Europa und Nordamerika. Immigrationspolitik und Integrationsprozesse in der Frühen Neuzeit, 1548–1787.* Frankfurt/Main, New York: Campus.

Malino, Frances (1978). *The Sephardic Jews of Bordeaux: Assimilation and Emancipation in Revolutionary and Napoleonic France.* University of Alabama: The University of Alabama Press.

Melammed, Renée Levine (2004). *A Question of Identity. Iberian Conversos in Historical Perspective.* Oxford, New York: Oxford University Press.

Motley, John L. (1898). *The Rise of the Dutch Republic*, 4 vols. London: Harper.

Muchnik, Natalia (2002). Du judaïsme au catholicisme: les aléas de la foi au XVIIIe siècle. *Revue Historique*, 623, 572–609.

Muchnik, Natalia (2005). Des intrus en pays d'inquisition: présence et activités des juifs dans l'Espagne du XVIIe siècle. *Revue des Études juives*, 164/1–2, 119–156.

Po-Chia Hsia, Ronnie (2002). Introduction. In Ronnie Po-chia Hsia and Henk Nierop (eds.). *Calvinism and Religious Toleration*, 27–52. Cambridge: Cambridge University Press.

Rabaut Saint-Etienne, Jean-Paul (1787). *Justice et nécessité d'assurer en France un état légal aux protestants*. No place: Ausbourg.

Samuel, Edgar (1988–1990). The readmission of Jews to England in 1656 in the context of English Economy policy. *Transactions of the Jewish Historical Society of England* (TJHSE), 31, 153–169.

Samuel, Edgar (2006). *At the End of the Earth. Essays on the History of the Jews in England and Portugal.* London: The Jewish Historical Society of England.

Schorsch, Jonathan, Portmanteau Jews: Sephardim and Race in the Early Modern Atlantic World. In David Cesarini (ed.). *Port Jews. Jewish Communities in Cosmopolitan Maritime Trading Centres, 1550–1950*, 59–74. London, Portland/OR: Frank Cass.

Schorsch, Jonathan (2004). *Jews and Blacks in the Early Modern World.* New York: Cambridge University Press.

Sorkin, David (1999). The Port Jew: Notes Toward a Social Type. *Journal of Jewish Studies*, 50/1, 87–97.

Sorkin, David (2002). Port Jews and the Three Regions of Emancipation. In David Cesarini (ed.). *Port Jews. Jewish Communities in Cosmopolitan Maritime Trading Centres, 1550–1950*, 31–46. London, Portland/OR: Frank Cass.

Studemund-Halévy, Michael (2005). Les aléas de la foi. Parcours d'un jeune Portugais entre église et synagogue. In Birgit E. Klein and Christiane E. Müller (eds.). *Memoria – Wege jüdischen Erinnerns. Festschrift für Michael Brocke zum 65. Geburtstag*, 363–382. Berlin: Metropol.

Swetschinski, Daniel M. (2004), *Reluctant Cosmopolitans. The Portuguese Jews of Seventeenth-Century Amsterdam.* Oxford, Portland/OR: The Littman Library of Jewish Civilization.

Van Ruymbeke, Bertrand (forthcoming 2009). From France to *le Refuge*. The Huguenots' multiple identities. In Susanne Lachenicht and Kirsten Heinsohn (eds.). *Diaspora Identities. Exile, Nationalism and Cosmopolitanism in Past and Present.* Frankfurt/Main: Campus.

Weiner, Gorden M. (1994). Sephardic philo- and anti-Semitism in the early modern era: the Jewish adoption of Christian attitudes. In Richard H. Popkin and Gordon M. Weiner (eds.). *Jewish Christians and Christian Jews: from the Renaissance to the Enlightenment*, 189–214. Dordrecht: Kluwer.

Yogev, Gedelia (1978). *Diamonds and Corals: Anglo-Dutch Jews and Eighteenth-Century Trade.* Leicester: Leicester University Press.

From France to *le Refuge*: The Huguenots' multiple identities

Bertrand Van Ruymbeke

While the question of whether the Huguenots can be considered a diaspora has been dealt with elsewhere (Van Ruymbeke 2007, 155–69) this contribution first discusses what French historians call *le Refuge huguenot* from a straightforward historical perspective and then offers a reflection on the various Huguenot identities and their mutations through space and time.

The Characteristics of the Huguenot Diaspora

The Huguenot Refuge, what it was and what it was not: In a very empiric way, I would like to begin with facts and numbers. The Huguenot exodus was born out of a paradox. It is one of the largest dispersions in early modern Europe yet, unlike the Jews in 1492 and the Moriscos in 1609 both groups forcefully driven out of Spain, the Huguenots were not expelled from France. This is an oddity typical of *ancien régime* France. In the 1685 Edict of Fontainebleau or Edict of Revocation, which replaced the 1598 Edict of Nantes – through which the Huguenots had been guaranteed civil, religious, juridical, and political privileges – the Protestants (except for pastors who were instructed to leave the kingdom within two weeks) were denied the *ius emigrandi* or the right to emigrate. This was in total contradiction with the 1555 Peace of Augsburg consensus which implicitly governed the application of its central rule »one king, one faith«. Whereas religious minorities had since then benefited from the right (rather than from an invitation) to leave a state, principality, or city, the French monarchy chose to close its borders, except for a brief period when it was thought, based on a strange psychology, that if the borders were opened the Huguenots would stay. Needless to say this measure was quickly repealed (Cottret 1998; Labrousse 1990 [1985]; Goodbar 1998).

Beyond their inherent discrepancies, there was nonetheless a rationale behind royal policies. The crown wished to eradicate Protestantism but not rid the kingdom of its Protestant subjects. These are entirely different objectives. Perhaps the monarchy was aware of the economic weight of this proportionately small population, roughly 700,000 people or 4 percent of the total population of France then estimated at twenty million people (Benedict 1991; Mours 1966). An influence nonetheless exaggerated by members of refugee communities in the eighteenth century, in the wake of Maréchal Vauban's 1689 *Mémoire pour le rappel des Huguenots*, and Protestant historians in the nineteenth and early twentieth centuries who wanted to prove that the Revocation was the starting point and main cause of France's long term economic decline (Yardeni 1993; de Vauban 1998). The monarchy's goal was the religious unification of the kingdom since in the pre-modern worldview toleration was a weakness, the sign of an inability to suppress otherness. Eradicating Protestantism was a proof of strength and of political coherence. The dual religious arrangement put in place at the end of the religious wars by Louis XIV's grandfather, Henry IV, had been a compromise reached by a much-weakened monarchy eager to lay the grounds of a lasting peace.

Therefore, as Emmanuel Le Roy Ladurie once put it: »[if] in terms of abstract morality, the Revocation proved reprehensible…it can [however] be vindicated if we stick to the requirements of Church, King and Country unity.« (Le Roy Ladurie 1991, 298). This essay is not a vain effort to justify the Revocation simply because the 87-year old Edict of Nantes should have been granted the respect that seniority calls for and because the Revocation, beyond the individual violence that it provoked, destabilised France and Europe, caused more problems that it was meant to solve and, in the long term, resuscitated a religion that was slowly dying its own death. It was therefore a total failure even from the standpoint of the monarchy.

Persecution and emigration were not new phenomena in Huguenot history. In the sixteenth century, following the 1572 Saint-Bartholomew's Day massacres, many Huguenots fled to neighbouring countries and cities. However, two factors made the post-1685 exodus unique to them (and to France): the number of fugitives involved and the fact that the Revocation eliminated the Huguenot churches (if not Protestantism as a whole) so that Huguenot exiles had nothing to return to. Estimates of the numbers of refugees have evolved tremendously since contemporaneous estimates. Even today, it appears, that each time one opens a book on the subject one runs into a new estimate. Discarding groundless figures of several millions mentioned in the nineteenth century, recently, and especially since the publication in 1960 of American historian Warren Scoville's study on the Revocation and French economic development, estimates have oscillated between 160,000 and 200,000. The trend goes downward though (Scoville 1960; Butler 1985).

In *Memory and Identity. The Huguenots in France and the Atlantic Diaspora*, Willem Frijhoff, who wrote a piece on the Huguenots in the Netherlands, quoted the figure as being 35,000, thus cutting by half the estimate that had been circulating until then (Frijhoff 2003). Conversely (but it does not compensate this numeric loss) in my own work I have increased Jon Butler's numbers of refugees who settled across the Atlantic by at least a thousand (Butler 1985, 47–9; Van Ruymbeke 1999, 195–7). Clearly, figures are evolving and more work – especially of demographic nature –needs to be done on the *Refuge*. At any rate, 180,000 refugees, to use a median estimate, is a large number and represents about a quarter of pre-Revocation France's Huguenot population. Yet, this figure means that the vast majority of Huguenots remained and converted. Protestantism, however, survived and by the end of the eighteenth century it had reached its pre-Revocation numbers although in proportion it weighed much less than a century before since France's population in the meantime had jumped from 20 to 27 million people.

Who left and for where? To put it briefly four main parameters conditioned the choice to escape: geography, occupation, education, and finances. Huguenots living in border areas or near a port – especially along the Atlantic Ocean and the English Channel – had better access to foreign destinations. Additionally, Huguenots who lived in predominantly Catholic provinces, such as Brittany or Burgundy, where resistance was nearly impossible left whereas those from overwhelmingly Protestant regions, such as Languedoc, remained. The figures are striking: 58 percent of the Huguenots in Brittany and 59 percent in Burgundy left while we have only 6 percent in the Cévennes and 8 percent in Languedoc who departed their native lands. The number of refugees was therefore inversely proportional to the size of the local Huguenot population (Butler 1985).

Gradually, in the 1660s and 1670s, the monarchy banned or severely limited the practice of certain occupations by Protestants who therefore had to leave (or convert) simply to survive economically. In other cases certain occupations facilitated escapes. Merchants, for example, whose wealth was in liquidity consigned a high volume of merchandise abroad so that the money gained from the sales remained there. Huguenots whose assets consisted of estates did not have this opportunity since selling a manor raised too much attention among Catholic neighbours and local religious and royal authorities and was rapidly banned by the monarchy anyway. Artisans, especially surgeons, apothecaries, and goldsmiths, easily found employment abroad, so easily in fact that their economic prosperity led to riots in various places. Education and wealth also facilitated escapes as Huguenots with geographic knowledge and contacts abroad and Huguenots who had studied or spent some time in a foreign country knew how to escape and where to go.

Money, of course, was necessary to hire guides or to purchase maps with roads along which was shown the location of inns whose owners could be trusted. The arrest and subsequent interrogation of a guide named Pierre Michaut in 1715 reveal that the eight fugitives in the group paid £6 sterling per person – the equivalent of half of the annual salary of an artisan – to be guided out of Poitou, across eastern Brittany to the island of Jersey. The male fugitives were condemned to the galleys and the females to prison and all were fined £75 sterling. The guide was hanged (Maillard 1900). Finally, personal factors such as age and family dynamics – for example who in the family was instructed to remain behind in order to maintain the estate – also played a role.

Origin and Uses of the Term *Refuge*

What is meant by the term *Refuge*? The word, used in the sense of dispersion, was coined by the earliest historian of the Huguenot exodus, Charles Weiss in his *Histoire des réfugiés huguenots de la Révocation à nos jours* published in 1853. It is specific to French historiography but it is an imported usage. In fact the very use of the terms »refuge« and »refugees« reveals (and this is not a minor point) that the Huguenot dispersion has been neglected by French historians and its history has been written first and primarily from the perspective of the countries of the *Refuge* (Weiss 1853; Birnstiel 2001, introduction 15–25). This trend is best illustrated by the well-known works of Jean-Pierre Erman and Pierre Chrétien Frédéric Reclam on Brandenburg-Prussia (1782–1799), Samuel Smiles on the British Isles (1870) and

Charles Washington Baird on America (1885). To a certain extent, leaving aside the issues of the prejudice usually felt towards a minority group and the ethnocentric tendencies of French historians, this neglect can be justified since while the Revocation belongs to the history of France, the exodus belongs to that of the British Isles, Germany, the Netherlands, Switzerland, South Africa and the United States.

The term »refugee« was used at the time of the dispersion. In England and in its colonies, local populations and authorities spoke or wrote about the »French refugees«, not about Huguenots or French Calvinists. This remark brings me to my second point, that of Huguenot identities, and I will start with the easiest topic, which concerns the question of semantics. The word »refugee« has two important implications. It implies, first, that the Huguenots were victims of Catholic absolutism and left France seeking refuge or protection and, second, as we have seen, that their migration has been described from the perspective of the host societies, those who welcomed them. Seventeenth-century French authorities labelled them fugitives, not refugees, as in the *»Listes des fugitifs«* that were compiled by the *intendants* (provincial administrators). Thus the use of the words »*Refuge*« and »*réfugié*« reflects the fact that their history was written by historians outside of France, sometimes by descendants of refugees. What is interesting though is that these terms became accepted in France itself, although to French historians these displaced Huguenots would rather have been *émigrés* or *fugitives* that is, anything but refugees.

Since the work of Jules Michelet in the 1860s, the Huguenot diaspora has been compared to the other large early modern migration out of France, that of the royalists at the time of the French Revolution. In the historiography, these refugees have been called *émigrés* and their migration *l'émigration*. The term *émigré*, like the word *réfugié*, appeared contemporaneously to its associated migration. As early as 1791, revolutionary authorities compiled lists of *émigrés*, just as the monarchy had done with the Huguenots, but the term remained. Originally, an *émigré* was simply one who left, who emigrated, the French language making a distinction between *émigrer* (from the perspective of the country of departure) and *immigrer* (from that of the host country), but after 1793, in the context of the Franco-British war, the word took on a negative connotation. The *émigrés* were those who not only refused to support the revolutionary cause and opposed *les patriotes* but they were also those who abandoned France in the midst of a war. The difference between the *émigré* and the refugee is therefore not just one of geo-historiographic perspective but reflects a subjective and moral perception of their experience. The *émigrés* were migrants who voluntarily left France while the Huguenots were victims of an absolutist regime (Van Ruymbeke 2006a).

Republican Jules Michelet captured the essence of this biased perceptive dichotomy when he wrote: »The émigrés of [17]93 wanted to save their lives, those of 1685 their souls« (Michelet 1985, 40). In other words, the *émigré*'s flight was neither heroic nor lofty as opposed to that of the Huguenot. Yet there is more to this distinction. By resisting absolutism and intolerance, the Huguenot acted as a precursor to modernity while the *émigré* opposed it by rejecting the Revolution. The *émigré* dreamed of a return to *ancien régime* political and socio-cultural practices, in contrast to the Huguenot who anticipated the changes brought about by the Enlightenment while aspiring to greater tolerance and religious diversity. This biased perception is still alive today in France where Protestantism is perceived as a source of French republicanism.

Ironically, however, the *émigrés*, unlike the Huguenots, were true refugees in the sense that their migration turned out to be temporary. As soon as they felt it was safe to return to France, they did, and most of them were back long before the eventual Restoration of the Bourbons in 1815. Conversely, the Huguenot refugees turned out to be migrants or *immigrés* as they integrated into the various host societies that welcomed them. Perhaps this fact also explains why the Huguenots (refugees) and their migration (Refuge) are still characterised in terms of where they settled rather than by their national origin. Oddly enough, in the United States the Huguenot ancestor is often called the *émigré* but here the word is stripped of its French historiographic meaning. The *émigré* is the one who made the consequential decision to leave France and cross the Atlantic and who founded a dynasty in the New World.

The Multiple Facets of Huguenot Identity

Let us now move beyond semantics and disentangle the threads of Huguenot identities: those of the days, contemporaneous to the migration, and those constructed through time as a by-product of the memory of the migration. For clarity's sake I would suggest to call the first »historic identities« and the second »memorial identities«. I see the former as a series of superimposed circles. The Huguenots were before all subjects of a French monarch and lived in the kingdom of France. As we know subjectship more than nationhood was the main parameter of collective identity in *ancien régime* societies. The Huguenots did not share the monarch's religion and therefore remained outside the national religious body. Yet, in a fascinating twist, their gallicanism, expressed in the Protestant opposition to the Pope, ironically supported France's religious autonomy within Catholicism, while their steadfast loyalty to the monarchy, arising from the provisions of the Edict of Nantes which were guaranteed solely by the Crown, reinforced their Frenchness. Seventeenth-century Huguenot writers always stressed that they were good subjects, and indeed their support of young Louis XIV during the noble and parliamentary rebellion, known as the *Fronde*, which threatened the monarchy in the 1650s, is a telling proof of it. Yet, the Huguenots, since the 1550s, had been torn between their religious and political identities. They were good subjects to be sure but subjects of a different sort nonetheless. Their Calvinism made them suspect in the eyes of Catholic polemists.

Huguenots were continuously suspected of harbouring republican ideas and entertaining ties to foreign Calvinists such as the dreaded English Puritan and Presbyterian regicides. In fact, the opposite was true. Whereas in the sixteenth century the Huguenots had enjoyed strong ties to English and Dutch Protestants who militarily and financially helped them during the Wars of Religion, in the following century, the Huguenots, lost in a Catholic sea, became gradually isolated from the rest of Protestant Europe. This was partly a consequence of their specific situation, as a Protestant minority group in a powerful Catholic absolutist state, and partly due to specific royal prohibitions such as Louis XIII's decision to prevent the Huguenot delegates from attending the 1619 pan-Calvinist Synod of Dort, which ruled on major doctrinal issues. Historians need to keep this isolation in mind when addressing the thorny issue of Huguenot conformity to the Church of England (Labrousse 1987, 143–57).

Culturally there is no doubt that the Huguenots, as Elisabeth Labrousse put it, »were proud to be French« and, in a spirit of Gallican arrogance, considered foreigners »with tacit condescension«. Indeed one must be careful not to let differences eclipse similarities. Beyond their Calvinism, the Huguenots were fundamentally *»des Français comme les autres«*. Although regional divisions in ancien regime France – while real – must not be exaggerated, Huguenots, like their Catholic counterparts, first belonged to a region or province. This is our second circle. Although the Huguenots, except in the mountainous Cévennes and parts of rural Poitou, tended to be educated and urbane and had thus access to French, the language of power, they could usually also speak a language other than French (Breton or Provençal for example) or speak certain variations of French. They were all deeply attached to specific cultural practices which they shared with their Catholic neighbours. They were well versed in the history of their provinces and the most prestigious of them belonged to local or provincial dynasties and were involved in local politics. Even in predominantly Catholic provinces or municipalities the Huguenots were truly part of their communities. At the national level their distinct religion kept them out of the political game but at the local level, at least up until the late 1670s when persecution intensified, they remained major actors.

Because in *ancien régime* France conversion to Protestantism was often an individual initiative, Huguenots kept strong kinship ties with Catholics in their communities. They often attended Catholic baptisms and marriages although afterward they had to repent before the elders of their churches. An anecdote, reported by Elisabeth Labrousse, well illustrates this Huguenot-Catholic community life. One Sunday four individuals were caught playing cards in a small southern town. Among them were the daughter of the pastor, the wife of a former elder, and the village Catholic priest! (Labrousse 1990, 71). The intensification of the legal and physical persecution in the late 1670s and a royal policy that encouraged informing put a heavy strain on these amicable Huguenot-Catholic relations, although, as it is reported in escape accounts, fugitives were sometimes helped by Catholic neighbours who shared with the Huguenots a distrust of both clerical and royal authorities.

The migration involved an inevitable mutation of identities. The Huguenots became French. This is a phenomenon experienced by all those who have travelled abroad. The implication of this does not mean that you cannot be French in France, but the difference is that in France Frenchness is a collectively self-fashioned identity implicitly shared but rarely mentioned except in times of war or national celebrations. But once abroad Frenchness suddenly becomes a primary identity according to parameters that travelling or expatriated French individuals do not control and sometimes are not even aware of. This is what is called an ascribed identity. Foreigners are identified with a series of cultural traits associated with their countries of origin. Historiography, as shown by the abusive association of the terms »French Huguenots« [for in that case should not we talk of Belgian or Swiss Huguenots ?], has blurred these differences and has confused Huguenots, Swiss Calvinists, and Walloons but at the time of the migration the refugees as well as the members of the host societies knew that a Swiss was not a Huguenot or a Walloon. The 1697 South Carolina naturalisation list, for example, was unambiguously entitled »Liste des Français et des Suisses«. (Van Ruymbeke 2006b, 177–84). Jean-François Gignilliat, a Swiss from Neuchâtel, who moved to South Carolina, informed his brother in a 1690 letter that »he married a French demoiselle«, congratulated himself on being considered »the wealthiest foreigner in the area«, and thought that being Swiss contributed to this status, writing that »the English seemingly like our nation« (Cohen and Yardeni 1988). Likewise, Paul l'Escot, the minister of the Charleston Huguenot Church, in a letter addressed to his former theology professor at Geneva, wrote that although born in Nevers, France, he »could pass as a Genevois« in Paris. It would be interesting to know what cultural and linguistic transformations enabled him to switch identities from that of a Huguenot to that of a Genevois.[1]

The case of the Walloons is more complex due to the ever-shifting borders between northern France and the Spanish Netherlands or present-day Belgium. Wars, territorial losses and conquests meant that one could almost literally one night fall asleep a Walloon and the day after wake up a Huguenot or vice-versa! More seriously, a Huguenot from Artois must have been culturally close to a Walloon from Brabant as shown by the amazingly ethnically homogeneous Huguenot-Walloon community of New Paltz founded in 1678 in upstate New York. One could say that, subjectship aside, the cultural differences between a Walloon and a Huguenot could be less than between two Huguenots from geographically diverse and culturally distinctive French provinces, such as Brittany and Languedoc (Van Ruymbeke 2005a).

Huguenot refugees had therefore a dual identity: they were French in their interaction with their host societies and other Francophone migrants but identified themselves with their provinces or communities of origin among themselves. The migration, a time of rupture and dislocation *par*

1 Eugène de Budé, (ed.), Lettres inédites adressées de 1686 à 1737 à Jean-Alphonse Turretini, théologien genevois, 3 vols., Paris, Librairie de la Suisse française, 1887, »Paul l'Escot à J-A Turretini, La Haye, le 14 mars 1698«, vol. 2., p. 220.

excellence, led to a cultural and social mixing or »brassage«, to use Myriam Yardeni's phrase, that would have been impossible to experience on the same scale in France (Yardeni 1985, 47). Marriages are a good indicator of this mixing, not so much in large European cities where many Huguenots congregated, but rather in isolated communities in Ireland, Germany, and especially in North America and South Africa where francophone matrimonial markets were tight. Although local familial alliances were maintained through the migration, either by leaving France together or by regrouping in a pre-determined place once abroad, the *Refuge* offers many examples of social mismatches, called in France *mésalliances* and culturally exotic, not to say unheard of, unions. In my own research, for example, I found a nobleman marrying a former maid and a Norman marrying a woman from Languedoc, and another Norman marrying somebody from Dauphiny in the Alps (Van Ruymbeke 2006b, 89). This inter-provincial mixing, with cultural and linguistic dimensions, must be taken into consideration when discussing the issue of integration into the host society. In the *Refuge* this Franco-French *brassage*, a sort of integration within the exile group itself, turned out to be a preliminary step to the integration into the host societies and not a way to resist it, although it may have been one at first. Parodying Michel Guillaume Jean de Crévecoeur's eighteenth-century portrait of the melting-pot in the United States with the phrase »The American: this new man«, one could talk about »the Huguenot refugee, this new man« (Crèvecœur 1782, letter no.3)

In the Refuge one also finds Huguenots of foreign origin. There are few of them but they present fascinating cases in terms of identity. Jacques Boyd, for example, was born in La Rochelle but moved with his family to Bordeaux. The Boyds were originally from Scotland and became rich merchants. At the time of the Revocation Jacques and his brother Jean first fled to England and then to South Carolina. There, Jacques wrote a letter to a sister back in Scotland in which he totally identified himself with the Huguenots since he mentioned »*les Anglais*« (a term which when used by foreigners must be taken in the generic sense of British) and eventually led a petition of Huguenots for naturalisation. Although he was only a first generation Frenchman on his father's side, his Scottish name and his knowledge of English distinguished him from the rest of the group (Ressinger 2008; Hancock 1997, 46–8). In a similar vein Canadian historian John Bosher has warned that what may seem in the *Refuge* to be ethnically exogamous marriages are actually a continuation of bi-national marriages common in French ports between daughters and sons of merchants (Bosher 1995). In other words, within his community, a Huguenot could and did marry a foreigner, which means that exogamous marriages are not necessarily a consequence of the migration.

An incident involving Huguenots and pirates from the Caribbean, which we know only through the prism of an *intendant's* account, offers another case of multiple identities. In 1686 French privateers from Saint-Domingue, presumably from the notorious pirates' heaven of the *Ile de la Tortue* on the northern coast of present-day Haiti, called at Charleston, supposedly at the invitation of the local population, who, it is true, in the first years of the existence of the colony relied on an illegal trade with pirates for tools and species. In this case though, the three ships were looted. The settlers »wanted to throw themselves onto the French simply because they were Catholic«, but the crews were saved through the intervention of »le Sieur de la Chabocière, *gentilhomme* and refugee« before »the governor sent them back to Saint-Domingue after stripping them of their weapons«. This incident reveals that the buccaneers were under attack not because they were pirates or French (i.e potential enemies) but – and apparently exclusively – because they were Catholic. This must have been reassuring to the Huguenot refugees who felt uncomfortable when established in a country at war with France and therefore needed to show evidence of an unequivocal loyalty to their hosts, just as they had had to do in France before the Revocation, as we have seen. Nonetheless this altercation also reveals how blurred lines of identity were since le Sieur de la Chabocière rescued the pirates precisely because they were French without minding their being Catholic.[2]

This brings me to my last factor of historical Huguenot identity: their religious identity. Huguenots were Calvinists. Their church life was based on the 1559 Paris *Discipline* and the 1571 La Rochelle *Confession of Faith*. It was inspired by the teachings, writings, and correspondence of Calvin, but it had its own structure and history. Abroad, and in England especially, the refugees evolved in a pluri-Protestant world, something that was quite new to them. Before the Revocation the Huguenots looked at English religious history from a distance. As American historian Erskine Clarke puts it, »the bitter divisions that had separated republicans and royalists in Britain were not part of their experience« and »when they looked at the Church of

2 » Lettre au marquis de Seigneulay « (14.June 1687), Bibliothèque Nationale, ms. NAF, Arnoul 21334, fol. 194. For the South Carolina context see (Van Ruymbeke 2006b, 181–3).

England they saw, after all, a historic Protestant church whose classic documents reflected the influence of Geneva.« (Clarke 1996, 164). Ironically the Huguenots shared the distrust, and towards certain groups such as the Quakers even the contempt, that French Catholics – and high Anglicans for that matter – felt toward the various Protestant sects. Pastor Paul L'Escot explained to his Swiss correspondent that the Quaker meeting house was but »a wretched hut« and that the Anglicans »*mettent bien de la difference entre nous et les dissidents*«.[3] In other words they did not confuse the Huguenots with the Dissenters.

The Huguenot Refuge in National Memories

The aspect of Huguenot identity I would like to discuss now is the one which was fashioned over the centuries. In my introduction to *Memory and Identity* I discussed the extraordinary ease with which the group has adapted to a myriad of memorial environments and has collectively espoused various national myths *pour le meilleur et pour le pire*. Nowhere is this capacity more astonishing than in South Africa. There, Huguenot legacy helped define the *Afrikaner* identity and the *Refuge* retroactively became another Great Trek. Although the Huguenots constituted less than 15 percent of their ethnic makeup, twentieth-century *Afrikaners* »spoke of all the *Afrikaans* settlers as having settled in South Africa to escape religious persecution«. However, in post-apartheid South Africa, Nelson Mandela praised the »French Huguenots [who] brought [to the Cape of Good Hope] a culture enriched by their own struggle for human rights«.

In the United States Huguenot memorial identity is very sophisticated. The Huguenot refugee is first a pioneer, a founder. This gives his descendants tremendous prestige by making them part of what American historian Ann Abrams, who studied the rival myths of Pocahontas and of the *Mayflower*, describes as an aristocracy of anteriority. (Abrams 1999, 12). Additionally the Huguenots were Calvinists who fled a Catholic absolutist state. Their experience admirably fits the historical canons of Protestant America, the master narrative of the »city upon a hill«. In other words the

3 »L'Escot to Turrettini« (Charleston, 1.March 1703), Bibliothèque Publique et Universitaire de Genève, Archives Tronchin, 81, fol. 202 front.

Huguenots were French Puritans and the *Richmond*, the ship that brought the first of them to South Carolina in 1680, a true *Mayflower*.

As an early twentieth-century American chronicler wrote, the Huguenot was »a French Puritan, in substance identical to the English Puritans [and] not fundamentally different from a French Catholic, except that he averaged higher« (Anonymous 1912, 29). Could it be that the Huguenots were the best France could offer? This feeling of superiority attached to Calvinism is to be interpreted as an adaptation of the theological concept of election, reinforced in the United States by the fact that the transatlantic migration is perceived as a process of selection. Election, persecution, selection, and migration are therefore the pillars of the Huguenot memorial identity in the New World (Van Ruymbeke 2003).

But this is not all. The Huguenot has managed to marry two antinomic American cultural traditions: that of the Puritan, symbolising the North, and of the Cavalier, that is the Southern planter *Gone with the Wind* style. Since he was French the Huguenot could only be a noble. This is a fantasised association that I call Frenchness and *noblesse*. In his successful dime novel, entitled *North and South*, John Jakes typically made the ancestor of the Southern character a fictional noble Huguenot fleeing his *château* in the Loire Valley. The Huguenot is a Puritan therefore in popular imagination. He is a pious, honest, hard-working Calvinist but since he is also French he has class and since he has Latin blood, he enjoys life and has exquisite taste as well as savoir-vivre. He truly is a Puritan aristocrat. In South Carolina – and to some extent in Virginia as well – this aspect of Huguenot identity went through remarkable mutations. After being a settler in the 1680s, he became a South Carolina planter in the mid-eighteenth century, then a patriot in the 1780s, then a Southerner to eventually become an American after the Civil War (Van Ruymbeke 2005b).

In the *Refuge* therefore the Huguenots are definitively on the winning side of history. This is due to their chameleonic faculty to blend in various cultural environments. Yet, in France there is also a Huguenot myth. As Michelet anticipated, there the Protestants are associated with modernity, with secular republicanism, la *République laïque* dear to nearly all French people (Cottret 2003). Therefore, in the *Refuge* but also in France, the Huguenots eventually integrated into mainstream society. This integration, and this will be my concluding thought, must be seen as part of an identity changing process, an evolution, not as a sudden transformation.

Works cited

Abrams, Ann U. (1999). *The Pilgrims and Pocahontas. Rival Myths of American Origin.* Boulder, Colorado: Westview Press.

Anonymous (1912). *No title.* Transactions of the Huguenot Society of South Carolina 19, 29.

Benedict, Philip (1991). *The Huguenot Population of France, 1600–1685: The Demographic Fate and Customs of a Religious Minority.* Philadelphia: American Philosophical Society.

Birnstiel, Eckart (ed.). (2001). *La diaspora des huguenots. Les réfugiés protestants de France et leur dispersion dans le monde (XVIe–XVIIIe siècles).* Paris: Honoré Champion.

Bosher, John F. (1995). Huguenot Merchants and the Protestant International in the Seventeenth Century. *William and Mary Quarterly*, 3rd series, 52, 77–102.

de Budé, Eugène (ed.). (1887). *Lettres inédites adressées de 1686 à 1737 à Jean-Alphonse Turretini, théologien genevois*, 3 vols. Paris: Librairie de la Suisse française.

Butler, Jon (1985). *The Huguenots in America. A Refugee People in New World Society.* Cambridge/Mass.: Harvard University Press.

Clarke, Erskine (1996). *Our Southern Zion. A History of Calvinism in the South Carolina Low Country, 1690–1990.* Tuscaloosa: University of Alabama Press.

Cohen, Robert and Miriam Yardeni (1988). Un Suisse en Caroline du Sud à la fin du XVIIe siècle. *Bulletin de la Société de l'Histoire du Protestantisme Français*, 134, 59–71.

Cottret, Bernard (1998). *1598. L'Édit de Nantes. Pour en finir avec les guerres de religion.* Paris: Perrin.

Cottret, Bernard (2003). Frenchmen by Birth, Huguenots by the Grace of God. Some Aspects of the Huguenot Myth. In Bertrand Van Ruymbeke and Randy J. Sparks (eds.). *Memory and Identity. The Huguenots in France and the Atlantic Diaspora*, 310–24. Columbia: University of South Carolina Press.

Crèvecœur, Michel Jean Guillaume (1782). *Letters from An American Farmer.* London: Thomas Davies.

Frijhoff, Willem (2003). Uncertain brotherhood. The Huguenots in the Dutch Republic. In Bertrand Van Ruymbeke and Randy J. Sparks (eds.). *Memory and Identity. The Huguenots in France and the Atlantic Diaspora*, 128–71. Columbia: University of South Carolina Press.

Goodbar, Richard L. (ed). (1998). *The Edict of Nantes: Five Essays and a New Translation.* Bloomington/IN: The National Huguenot Society.

Hancock, David (1997). *Citizens of the World. London Merchants and the Integration of the British Atlantic Community, 1735–1785.* Cambridge: Cambridge University Press.

Labrousse, Elisabeth (1987). Great Britain as Envisaged by the Huguenots of the Seventeenth Century. In Irene Scouloudi (ed.) *Huguenots in Britain and their French Background, 1550–1800*, 143–57. Totowa/NJ: Barnes & Nobles Books.

Labrousse, Elisabeth (1990) [1985]. *La révocation de l'édit de Nantes. Une foi, une loi, un roi?* Paris: Payot.

Le Roy Ladurie, Emanuel (1991). Afterword: Glorious revolution, shameful revocation. In Bernard Cottret. *The Huguenots in England. Immigration and settlement, c.1550–1700*, 298–305. Cambridge: Cambridge University Press.

Maillard, Th. (1900). Les routes de l'exil du Poitou vers les îles Normandes et l'Angleterre. Le guide Pierre Michaut. *Bulletin de la Société de l'Histoire du Protestantisme Français*, 49, 281–91.

Michelet, Jules (1985). De la Révocation de l'Edit de Nantes à la Guerre des Cévennes, reprint with an introduction by Paul Viallaneix [*from Histoire de France*, vol. 15 and 16, 1860]. Montpellier: Presses du Languedoc.

Mours, Samuel (1966). *Essai sommaire de géographie du protestantisme réformé français au XVIIe siècle*. Paris: Librairie Protestante.

Ressinger, Dianne W. (2008). The Boyd Family in Scotland, France, Carolina, St. Kitts, Ireland and England. *Transactions of the South Carolina Huguenot Society*, 112, 43–54.

Scoville, Warren (1960). *The Persecution of Huguenots and French Economic Development 1680–1720*. Berkeley: University of California Press.

Van Ruymbeke, Bertrand (1999). Le Refuge atlantique: la diaspora huguenote et l'Atlantique anglo-américain. In Guy Martinière, Didier Poton and François Souty (eds.). *D'un Rivage à l'Autre. Villes et Protestantisme dans l'Aire Atlantique (XVIe–XVIIe siècles)*, 195–204. Paris: Imprimerie Nationale.

Van Ruymbeke, Bertrand (2003). Minority Survival. The Huguenot Paradigm in France and the Diaspora. In Bertrand Van Ruymbeke and Randy J. Sparks (eds.). *Memory and Identity. The Huguenots in France and the Atlantic Diaspora*, 1–25. Columbia: University of South Carolina Press.

Van Ruymbeke, Bertrand (2005a). The Walloon and Huguenot Elements in New Netherland and Seventeenth-century New York: Identity, History, and Memory. In Joyce D. Goodfriend (ed.). *Revisiting New Netherland. Perspectives on Early Dutch America*, 41–54. Leiden: Brill.

Van Ruymbeke, Bertrand (2005b). Cavalier et Puritan. L'ancêtre huguenot au prisme de l'histoire américaine. *Diasporas. Histoire et Sociétés*, special issue *Généalogies rêvées*, 5, 5–22.

Van Ruymbeke, Bertrand (2006a). Réfugiés or Émigrés? Early Modern French Migrations to British North America and the United States. *Itinerario. International Journal on the History of European Expansion and Global Interaction*, 30:2, 12–32.

Van Ruymbeke, Bertrand (2006b). *From New Babylon to Eden. The Huguenots and Their Migration to Colonial South Carolina*. Columbia: University of South Carolina Press.

Van Ruymbeke, Bertrand (2007). Refuge or Diaspora? Historiographical reflections on the Huguenot dispersion in the Atlantic World. In Susanne Lachenicht (ed.). *Religious Refugees in Europe, Asia and North America (6th–21st century)*, 155–69. Hamburg: LIT.

Vauban, Sébastien Le Prestre, marquis de (1998). *Mémoire pour le rappel des Huguenots.* Carrières-sous-Poissy: La Cause.

Weiss, N. Charles (1853). *Histoire des réfugiés protestants de France depuis la révocation de l'Edit de Nantes jusqu'à nos jours.* 2 vols. Paris: Charpentier.

Yardeni, Myriam (1985). *Le refuge Huguenot.* Paris: Presses Universitaires de France.

Yardeni, Myriam (1993). Naissance et essor d'un mythe: la Révocation de l'Édit de Nantes et le déclin économique de la France. *Bulletin de la Société de l'Histoire du Protestantisme Français*, 139, 79–96.

»Apostles of the Nation and Pilgrims of Freedom«: Religious Representations of Exile in Nineteenth-Century Europe

Maurizio Isabella

A common feature of several European nationalisms of the first half of the nineteenth century was their development outside the territorial space of the state or states they aimed at creating. In order to fight for a democratic or liberal state that would recognise the nation as its founding principle, Italian, German and Polish patriots were often organised in national and trans-national associations and networks which were geographically »displaced«, but in constant contact with their countries of origin. After 1821, 1831 and 1848 Brussels, Paris and London hosted substantial exile communities of revolutionaries who organised themselves collectively and entertained intense intellectual exchanges (Freitag 2003). This context accounts for the intimate connection between the various patriotisms produced at the time, and for the existence of shared values, principles and discursive patterns among patriots of different national origins. It also fostered notions of international brotherhood and solidarity among nations, ideals mirrored in the numerous statements and associations that united patriots of different national origins between the 1820s and 1850s (Isabella 2008; Urbinati 2008). Finally, it produced brands of patriotism that reconciled national with universal claims. This, as has been observed, may well be true for most European nationalisms well beyond 1848. Vindications of the right to self-determination of nations were accompanied by the belief that national emancipation was a step towards the universal affirmation of freedom, equality and political participation (Varouxakis 2006). However, the experience of exile may well have enhanced the universalistic scope of the national aspiration developed abroad.

It is now widely accepted that post-revolutionary politics were characterised by new narrative and discursive practices that contributed to the advancement of its principles, ideals and values (Hunt 1984, 24–51). Ideas of nationhood and universality were thus vindicated through images, representations and a variety of linguistic conventions and rhetorical devices that aimed at making them compelling, persuasive and self-explanatory. It is a particular aspect of this new dimension of nineteenth-century political discourse that I intend to explore, namely the religious representations that the exiled patriots produced to describe themselves and their activities, and the contribution of such images to the definition of the relationship between nationality and universality. Their use of religious language and imagery was by no means exceptional or surprising. To the contrary, in the aftermath of the French revolution the political sphere adopted, endorsed and manipulated ideas, concepts and even rituals produced in the religious sphere which might by means of old, familiar ideas lend legitimacy to the new order. Despite their differing outcomes and ideological purposes, the language of Christianity and that of the revolutionary politics were thus merged, and the idea of national regeneration transformed into an inherently religious belief. This transfer from religion to politics took place at different levels and for different purposes. First, it entailed the political use of religious metaphors, symbols and rituals, which reinforced the rhetorical force of national and revolutionary programmes. Second, it resulted in the wholesale adoption of the Bible narrative by patriots to describe the entire history of their own nation and vindicate their destiny of liberation and regeneration. Francesca Sofia has recently observed that the use of the Bible by Italian patriots produced a »political re-writing of the Biblical tale« (Sofia 2001). The Bible became a metaphor for the condition of the entire Italian nation (Francia 2007). Finally, this transfer also produced a number of interesting attempts to reconcile, or even to merge faith, political freedom and progress with religion, individual rights and ideas of nationhood. These ideological processes, initiated in the revolutionary period in France and experienced also in other parts of the continent affected by the revolutionary wave, continued in the following decades, and in particular profoundly marked the political thought of the Romantic age. The re-appropriation of religious themes or ideas obviously did not take place without modification or adaptation, so that the ideas inspired by religion almost invariably took on new and original meanings. These combinations or adaptations also gave rise to a variety of Catholic liberalisms, or republicanisms inspired by an evangelical, or at least anti-papal and anti-despotic religiosity, exemplified by Felicité de Lamennais and Giuseppe Mazzini (Jaume 1997, 171–278; Traniello 1992, 324; idem 2007, 89–100).[1] As was the case with Saint-Simon and his followers, such transfer from religion to

1 On Mazzini's brand of Christian religiosity, influenced by Jansenism and Protestant Nonconformity, see Biagini 2008.

politics might also produce a new ideology concerned with the entire reorganisation of society and its productive forces based on the principles of industry, that drew its hierarchical structure from that of the Church, and was both authoritarian and hostile to the traditional, feudal forces of society. Saint-Simon aimed not only to found a new Church, but also a new religion that embodied the values of progress, and of the social and economic improvement of the whole social order (see at least J.L. Talmon 1960). Other patriots sometimes considered religion, and in particular Catholicism, to be the core value of their national communities, as was the case with the Italian Vincenzo Gioberti or the Polish Adam Mickiewicz. Moreover, many, if not all of the revolutionary leaders and charismatic intellectuals of the first decades of the nineteenth century, presented themselves as religious leaders, as Messiahs and bearers of a revealed truth about the world. This in turn had implications for the scope of their message, and for the universal nature of the national struggles they aspired to lead. As Talmon has written,

> »the deification of the nation necessitated the apotheosis of universal history and the oneness of mankind. Otherwise the uniqueness of the single nation was a freak, and could claim no absolute significance… Liberated nation-churches would combine into the Church universal«. (Talmon 1960, 29–30)

All of these processes represent different but equally important aspects of the sacralisation of politics that characterised the development of Western political culture in the nineteenth century (Gentile 2001; for the Risorgimento see also Levis Sullam 2004a). The religious descriptions of exile I intend to discuss hereafter, produced by a variety of leading European and Italian patriots, provide further evidence of these transfers from religion to politics, and demonstrate also the variety of ideological goals served by religious imagery. The best documented example of such linguistic and symbolic transfer has been that of the idea of martyrdom adopted to celebrate heroic death in modern political movements. Indeed, in the nineteenth century martyrdom for the fatherland became a powerful testimony of political faith, evidence of the importance of the cause and an example around which to develop patriotic and civic cults to found new political communities (Banti 2000; Riall 2008[2]). Admittedly, exile was often associated, along with imprisonment and death on the battlefield or in an insur-

2 The introduction to this edited volume presents an exhaustive discussion of the bibliography on the topic.

rection, with martyrdom (Isabella 2006). [3] However, what I intend to demonstrate is the importance of other religious metaphors more specifically suited to the experience of exile. In the nineteenth and twentieth centuries political movements had their own martyrs, but also needed Apostles and pilgrims.[4]

For exiled revolutionaries, the Christian tradition and the Holy Scriptures served as a constant inspiration through theology, Biblical narrations and venerable religious traditions. The Bible contained the memory of the Jews destined first to exile and slavery in Egypt, and then rescued thanks to the Exodus and the return to the Promised Land; the memory of captivity in Babylon, and also of their liberation, according to God's design to punish with proscription but also to offer salvation. A theology of exile could be drawn not only from the Old Testament, but also from the New, as Christ could be interpreted as the agent of the redemption of Israel, and his mission as the very end of the exile of his own people. The New Testament also suggested to modern readers, and in particular to the exiles, the powerful metaphor of the voyage of Apostles who preached the word of the Lord in the world (Scott 1997; Evans 1997). Finally, political emigration could refer to the ancient Christian tradition of Pilgrimage, with all its metaphoric meanings to explain its own experiences and justify its political activity. Pilgrimage is in fact a trip towards a sacred place and an extraordinary encounter with the divine. It is also both an individual and a collective trial and an act of penitence. While pilgrims broke with the stability of everyday life, they underwent spiritual regeneration and conversion, an experience which left an enduring mark upon them (Turner 1978; Bitton-Ashkelony 2005; Roppen and Sommer 1964; Eade and Sallnow 2000). These various models of religious voyage that turned away from, or lead to a new homeland and brought participants close to the divine, had the advantage of relating the personal experience of emigration to reassuring and comforting, although painful, experiences, linked as they were to the very history of Christianity and its rituals. I intend to discuss the huge influence

3 As demonstrated by Atto Vannucci, who writes at page 5 of *I martiri della libertà*, [1848] (I am quoting from the Florence edition of 1860):«The fruits of liberty which at home we are beginning to pick were sown and cultivated at terrible cost by our fathers and by our brothers. There is not a prison that has not been sanctified by the presence and by the sufferings of the most generous of men, not a foreign country that was not full of exiles, that did not see Italian travails, and in Italy there is not an inch of earth that was not steeped in the blood of the Martyrs of liberty«.

4 For the use of this religious terminology by Fascism see (Gentile 1996, esp. 109–121).

that these images and the theology of exile had on the self-representation of the community of exiles, whether Polish, Italian or Europe-wide. In particular, I will focus on two leading figures who played a crucial role in shaping ideas of exile, in order to demonstrate their impact on the Italian patriots of the *Risorgimento*: the French democrat Felicité de Lamennais and the Polish revolutionary Adam Mickiewicz. Finally, I shall consider the reaction of traditional Catholic culture to these re-appropriations by revolutionaries, liberals and democrats of religious images and of Christian theology. As I will demonstrate, the images of exile adopted, imitated and challenged across Europe helped to reinforce the intimate connection between ideas of nationality and those of universality. At the same time, however, they also point to the existence of a diversity of national models and a plurality of notions of universality linked to it.

Adam Mickiewicz and the Mission of the Pilgrims of the Polish Nation

In Paris since 1832 Adam Mickiewicz was, at the age of 33, one of the undisputed leaders of the Great Polish emigration that had left the country following the 1830–31 insurrection against Russian rule. Mickiewicz reached Paris after eight years of exile in Russia, Germany and Italy: he had joined the 1830 revolution only a few months after its outbreak. After the revolution a considerable number of Polish patriots flocked to Paris, by 1840 they numbered to more than 10,000.[5] Mickiewicz's patriotism was marked by a profound mysticism and by a determination to define the Polish Catholic heritage as central to Polish cultural and religious identity. The celebration of Polish Catholicism was accompanied by an hostility towardst the French revolutionary culture. With one of his most famous works, *The Books and the Pilgrimage of the Polish Nation* [1833], Adam Mickiewicz put the emigration at the centre of the patriotic discourse, setting it in a messianic and millenarian vision of history.[6] According to this vision humankind was ready to overcome the corrupt present and

5 On the Polish exiles in Paris see (Kramer 1988, 176–228).

6 The English version was published in London in 1833 with this title. The best analysis of the work is offered by (Koropeckyj 2001, 98–125) to which I am indebted for my brief discussion of the book.

return to an original Golden Age, in which all had lived in freedom, harmony and equality. During modern history, Mickiewicz argued, the Kings of the European nations had reneged upon Christianity, and replaced its values with those of commerce and of material pursuits. The resurrection of Poland, the only country to have maintained and protected its original moral and religious values, was to lead to the regeneration of the whole of Christianity, and thus to inaugurate an epoch of absolute harmony between people and nations, a new era of happiness for humanity. This interpretation identified the history of humankind with the doctrine of salvation, or soteriology.

What role was attributed to the exiles and what was the meaning of their experience in this vision of historical and religious progress? It was precisely the Polish exiles who would affect the transition from the current condition of slavery and exploitation of the nation towards its regeneration. The exiles, as representatives of the entire Polish national community, would lead it towards its liberation. Millenarianism always requires a Messiah as agent of salvation. According to the Millenarian tradition that inspired Mickiewicz, those who are marginalised, the humble and the meek would become key historical actors and executors of a divine plan. Likewise Mickiewicz described the *émigrés* as individuals living in poverty, as outcasts who were far from their fatherland. At the same time, they were also those chosen by God to announce and accomplish the inevitable resurrection of Poland and of the entire world, and to teach civilisation to foreigners. It is precisely in this context that the exiles were transformed into Pilgrims:

»But no Pole on his pilgrimage is called a wanderer, for a wanderer is a man straying without a goal; Nor is he an exile, for an exile is a man exiled by the decree of the government, but his government did not exile the Pole… meanwhile the Pole is called a pilgrim; and since he hath made a vow to journey to the holy land, the free country, he hath vowed to journey until he shall find it.« (Mickiewicz 1944, 380)

In the text Biblical references abounded: the Polish emigration was likened to the Exodus or as the voyage of the Chosen People to the Promised Land; the exiles were described not only as Pilgrims but also as Apostles sent by God to preach the Word, »as the Apostles among idolaters« (ibid., 403–4, 405). The religious dimension of the exiles' experience was also the literary style and structure of the *Book*, written as a sequence of Parables. As has recently been observed, the idea of mission employed by

Mickiewicz highlighted how their activity, rather then being the expression of a »rational duty« transformed the exiles into a »band of humble and faithful men« (Tilysinska 2004, 772). The Polish emigration in fact had a twofold mission, that of re-founding the homeland, and that of rescuing all of Christendom, since in Mickiewicz's vision national identity and Catholic religion, were deemed to coincide. It is precisely this aspect of the role of the exiles that likewise inspired the Italian patriots, and in particular Mazzini and Gioberti.

Félicité de Lamennais and the Exile of Humankind from God

A second and equally influential producer of religious, but politically resonant, representations of exile was Felicité de Lamennais. The intellectual debt owed by Lamennais to Mickiewicz is a matter of some controversy, yet there is no doubt that in 1834, when he wrote his best-selling *Paroles d'un croyant*, the French liberal was familiar with the work of the Polish exile: the 1833 French translation by Montalembert of the *Books and the Pilgrimage of the Polish Nation* included Lamennais' *Hymne à la Pologne* (Mickiewicz 1833). Although Lamennais had already vindicated the cause of the oppressed nation, and of the Poles in particular, in the pages of »L'Avenir«, a liberal Catholic review, it was only with his *Paroles* that he became unequivocally committed to freedom and democracy. The simple language and incantatory style of this remarkable book, modelled in a large part on the Gospels, earned it a vast readership, even among the working classes; indeed, it ran to seven editions, sold some 350,000 copies and was translated into several European languages (Verucci 1963, 236).

Lamennais' *Paroles* represented the culmination of a process initiated in 1830–31 with his articles in favour of the freedom of the press and the emancipation of the peoples. Rejecting the principle of authority represented by the Papacy and transforming the New Testament into a message of liberation for humankind in history, he broke away from the positions of the Catholic Church. For the Abbé, God had not in fact condemned humanity to evil: evil was not a law of God, but rather a moral disorder that could be remedied. Like Mickiewicz Lamennais espoused a Millenarian perspective: since progress was a divine law, and Christ had announced a message of freedom in history, then the restoration of the Kingdom of

God on earth was already underway. Thus emancipation from evil could be achieved on earth thanks to the teachings of Christ. Jesus was the messenger of the new alliance between God and the People. Lamennais, denouncing any barrier to the progression of humanity in the Earthly City, produced nothing less than a theology of liberation (Lambert 2001). It is thus unsurprising that a contemporary defined the *Paroles* as »the Marseillaise of Christianity«.[7] For Giuseppe Mazzini, the book »everywhere carried consolation and promise to the souls of the sorrowing and oppressed« (Mazzini 1891, 23). Although, as Lucien Jaume has acutely observed, the idea of sovereignty remained in Lamennais as a spiritual entity even in the democratic phase of his thought, being transposed, as it was, from the Pope and the Sovereigns to the Peoples, it nonetheless became an integral part of an earthly and democratic project (Jaume 1997, 201–204). He had thereby affected a complete secularisation of Christianity. The main character of the *Paroles* was, as in the case of Mickiewicz, the exile. Why? Because exile represents metaphorically the human existence on earth:

»The exile is everywhere alone. There are no friends nor brides, fathers nor brothers, save in the fatherland. The exile is everywhere alone. Cease to lament, poor exile; all men are banished like thee: all see fathers, brothers, brides, and friends pass away and vanish. Our Country is not here below; man seeks it here in vain; that which he takes for it is but a night's resting-place. He goes forth a wanderer upon earth. God guide the poor exile!« (Lamennais 1891, 111–112).

What was radically innovative, however, in Lamennais' interpretation of exile from God is that this status did not represent the necessary condition of human life, resulting from the distance of the Earth from God, to which only death and the ascent to the Kingdom of Heaven could put an end. On the contrary for Lamennais the Celestial City could be established on Earth, and the exile from God was solely due to the existence of poverty, despotism, oppression and inequality. In short, it was the exile of one who, wandering about the world

»will find a man who will drive you away, saying: This field is mine. After having passed through all lands you shall return, knowing that nowhere is there one poor little plot of round where your travailing wife, may bring forth her first-born, where you may rest after your labour, where, at last, your children may bury your bones as in a spot which is your own.« (Lamennais 1891, 53)

7 As the *Revue Encyclopédique* wrote (quoted by Verucci 1963, 239).

Lamennais called upon humankind to fight for freedom, as the exile is »a traveller seeking his fatherland. Walk not with downcast head: to know your road you must raise your eye« (ibid., 70).[8] As a consequence exile could be interpreted not only as a spiritual state, but also as the condition of men who were awaiting liberation from injustice, and had the right to fight to obtain it according to the teachings of Christ and his emancipatory project. The exiled man was thus encouraged to become a revolutionary, to rebel against his oppression and find again the place he merited on Earth. This same message provided the Italian exiles with a legitimation of their revolutionary activities.

Exile, democracy and the Risorgimento

Immediately after the publication of the works of Lamennais and Mickiewicz their interpretations of the theme of exile were embraced by several Italian patriots. The first to do so was Giuseppe Mazzini. The influence of these writers marked a new intellectual phase for Mazzini, characterised by the intensely religious and mystical tone of his writings. Inspired by Mickiewicz's vision of Poland, Mazzini turned Italy into another »martyr nation«. At the same time, his readings of Mickiewicz's texts coincided with a political turning point in his revolutionary career, one inaugurated by the organisation of »Young Europe«, founded in 1834. Through this federation of national associations, Mazzini aimed at providing his struggle for democracy and the emancipation of the peoples, to which »Young Italy« had represented his first strategic and organisational contribution, with a continental dimension. The establishment of democracy in Europe represented the extension of the programme he had sought to advance in Italy. However the failure of the conspiracies organised by »Young Italy« in 1833, and the defeat of the expedition in Savoy determined a change in his strategy that was also reflected in the objectives of the new pan-European federation. Now Mazzini, even more than he had already done with »Young Italy«, emphasised the educational function of the association, and underlined the need to vindicate by words, as well as

8 He also wrote: »Unless then you are resolved to fight without intermission, to endure all without wavering, never to be weary, never to yield, keep your fetters, and renounce the freedom of which you are not worthy« (Lamennais 1891, 77).

by deeds, the morality of the democratic cause. Significantly it was precisely in this period that Mazzini intensified his use of the word »Apostle«. The term, already employed in the documents of »Young Italy«, referred to the role the new recruits would play in advocating the ideas of national emancipation and in revealing the truth, thus bearing witness through their relentless activities and their willingness to sacrifice themselves to their faith in such beliefs (Sarti 1997, 80–83; idem 2008, 275–297).[9] The metaphor was in turn most probably borrowed from the Saint-Simonian school. The closest collaborators of its founder, who had cast himself as a Messiah and a new Christ, described their educational and propaganda activities as no less than the apostolic mission of the minority of wise men who were destined to enlighten humanity with their spiritual, social and scientific truths (Talmon 1960, 65–88, and esp. 70–77).

A pamphlet published in Lausanne in 1834 and entitled *Ils sont parti*, written just after a number of European exiles had been persecuted by the Swiss authorities, demonstrates the way in which Mazzini creatively reinvented the themes of the authors discussed above. The pamphlet seems to have enjoyed some success, as it was immediately translated into French and German, and then in Italian; it was republished in 1854 in *Italia e popolo*, and later several excerpts were used by Mazzini in his *Note Autobiografiche* (1861–66).[10] The tribute paid here to the two hundred young men, persecuted at the behest of the European powers, was designed first and foremost to galvanise the international group of *émigrés*, recently defeated in Savoy, and now driven by the Swiss government from Lausanne and forced to take refuge in mountain villages. On the cover of the pamphlet Mazzini quoted Lamennais's invocation »May God guide the poor exiles« from his *Paroles d'un croyant*. The whole article adopted and recast the language, images and ideas of both the French liberal and the Polish patriot:

»Yeah, they were but children [...] although a mothers' caresses, and the joy and consolations of hearth and home would no longer be theirs; they were children of a new world, of a new faith, and the Angel of exile had softly whispered to them some sweet and holy word of love, of universal brotherhood, of the soul's religion, of a radiant and powerful future [...] Then they set out, amidst the peoples, and whenever a sigh from oppressed and brave peoples had reached their ears, they

9 On the influence of Lamennais and Mickiewicz on Mazzini see also (Levis Sullam 2004b, 705–30).

10 The editorial vicissitudes are described in the introduction to (Mazzini 1908a, xli). Long excerpts were republished in (Mazzini 1944, 130–85).

had rushed to third aid; whenever a lament from oppressed and downtrodden people had pierced their hearts, they would say to them: rise up, and know your own strength [...] often they would ask for brotherly bread, and mud was thrown at them. But some trace of their pilgrimage would always remain, and even those who had cast them out would be astonished to feel in themselves, after their passage, some sort of change.« (Mazzini 1908b, 97–100)

Mazzini combined here Lamennais's concern for the progress and the democratic palingenesis of Europe, with Mickiewicz's emphasis upon the struggle for national emancipation. To the themes of the Apostolic mission and the pilgrimage Mazzini added a number of other Romantic elements. On the one hand he stressed the fact that exile severed family bonds, thus imparting pathos to his account of the refugees' fate, and demonstrating, according to a trope typical of *Risorgimento* literature, how such ties might stand in for patriotic affiliations.[11] On the other, he underlined the young age of the exiles, a motif present since the original founding of Young Italy – The youth of the community of *émigrés* served to project their message into the future, by emphasizing the fact that their ideals were destined to inaugurate a new phase in the history of humankind. By promoting the image of these young patriots from different nations, Mazzini also gave symbolic support to the transnational dimension of the rise of democracy and national awareness, according to the principles of Young Europe.

Mazzini's pages were not an isolated example in *Risorgimento* literature. Indeed, Lamennais and Mickiewicz became models for many Italian patriots when discussing the theme of exile and patriotism.[12] Consider, for instance, the case of Gustavo Modena, a follower of Mazzini, who in 1835 advocated the principles of European brotherhood of »Young Europe« (presented as a »declaration of faith«) in a pamphlet, the *Epistola di Lando ai Giovani italiani*, whose language was reminiscent of Lamennais and Mazzini. Modena denied that Heaven was the homeland of men, and called upon the exiles to fight, as »the kingdom of Truth will not come without war« (Modena [Paris 1835] 1957, 71). So too Tommaso Aniello in his *Inno all'Esule*, published in Turin in 1836, provides further evidence of the adoption and dissemination of increasingly familiar tropes regarding the relationship between freedom, patriotism and exile. From Mazzini's pam-

11 For a detailed discussion of the relationship betwen private feelings and public duty in the *Risorgimento* see (Ginsborg 2007, 5–67) and (Bonsanti 2007, 128–152).

12 A list of all the Italian imitators of Lamennais is provided by (Sancipriano 1973, 239–245).

phlet *Ils sont parti* Aniello had adopted the phrase »they are gone«, repeated at the beginning of each paragraph. The stylistic and literary model in either case was undoubtedly Lamennais' parables, whose patriotic and political content Aniello made even more explicit in his pamphlet. In the *Inno* the exile represents »the wretched and the oppressed … blessed by God«, and is the one who will announce the salvation of the whole fatherland. Taking his inspiration from the language of Lamennais, Aniello wrote that »The prayer of the exile will be the prayer of redemption addressed to the Christ of freedom« (Aniello 1836, 9). It is always the exile who teaches the people to love the homeland and to sacrifice themselves for it. In the wake of Mickiewicz the Italian people was likened to that of Israel, and the exiles to the Apostles of freedom (ibid., 17 and 25). Similarly, an anonymous publication, *L'esule e la sua patria*, published in Switzerland in 1848, celebrated the role of the Italian exile community in leading the nation. Exile was no longer simply the universal condition of humankind oppressed by despotism, but more specifically the status of the Italian nation itself, and of all those who had had to flee it in the face of repression. What remained of Lamennais was however the legitimation of the right to rebel against oppression:

»Rise up with one accord, O sons of the fields and of the factories; seize the hoes, your pikes in order to avenge your trampled rights; let us brandish the sword of vengeance, and all united, in serried ranks, ready for any trial be it even to the death, let us bear down upon the miserable dregs of tyranny accursed by men and struck down by God's wrath...« (Anon., 1848).[13]

Vincenzo Gioberti and the Civilizing Mission of the Italian Exiles

What I have highlighted so far has been the link that the religious representations of exile had created between emigration and national emancipation, and the role patriotic literature attributed to the exiles in advancing these ideals. A last, and no less important theme developed by the patriots was the relationship between the spreading of civilisation and exile. In the pages of *The Books and the Pilgrimage of the Polish Nation* Mickiewicz had un-

13 At p. 3 he quoted Lamennais »The exile is alone in the world«.

equivocally asserted that the exiles' true mission was to advocate the authentic Christian civilisation, and had warned them against being seduced by the ideas and values of foreign civilisations. For Mickiewicz, in fact, the exiles were »in a strange land in the midst of injustice, as travellers who in an unknown country fall into a pit. Some travellers fell into a wolves' pit…« (Mickiewicz 1944, 401). This attitude stemmed from his steadfast belief in the superiority of Polish culture, whose moral and spiritual values, identical to those of the most genuine Christianity, were bound to prevail in the world against French revolutionary ideas and the commercial, protestant values of England. Although still acknowledging the values of internationalism and universal brotherhood among the nations, Mickiewicz's notion of civilisation was predicated upon the superiority of the Poles.

Though possessed of an entirely different literary style, of all Italian patriots Vincenzo Gioberti most closely resembled Mickiewicz in his treatment of the relationship between exiles and foreign civilisations. Second only to Mazzini in fame, and no less influential in shaping new ideas of nationhood, Gioberti wrote some of the most popular books of the *Risorgimento*, namely the *Primato* (1843) and the *Prolegomeni del Primato* (1845), while exiled in Brussels. The central idea was that Italian nationhood had been shaped through history by the presence of the Papacy, which had gradually transferred the moral and religious values of Catholicism to the rest of the peninsula. For Gioberti the principles of modern civilisation stemmed from Catholicism, and thus civilisation, while accommodating the division between Church and state, as well as commercial values, was first and foremost religious in nature, according to an idea shared by the traditional Catholic culture (Menozzi 1986, 804). Italian primacy over the other nations stemmed precisely from the fact that Italy, through its being destined historically to host the centre of Christianity in Rome, embodied the universal values of religion and civilisation. This conception of nationality resulted in an anti-revolutionary programme, which envisaged the creation of an Italian confederation of existing monarchies under the presidency of the Pope (Traniello 2007, 73–7).[14]

These ideas were reflected also in Gioberti's vision of the mission attributed to the Italian exiles. Both in his *Primato Civile e Morale* and in his *Prolegomeni* the exiles are accorded an entire sections, whose content has not been the object of any scholarly investigation. For Gioberti »lo spatria-

14 On Gioberti's and moderates' idea of progress and civilisation see also (Romani 2006 21–50).

mento« (emigration from one's homeland) represented in history, from Moses onwards, a powerful vehicle for the dissemination of civilisation in the world. Gioberti had taken Israel and its history as a model for the destiny of all oppressed nations, and as an archetype of the very principle of nationality. Thus the narration of the destiny of the Jewish people could also be adopted to describe the Italian nation which, like the Jewish one, had resisted for centuries despite foreign oppression. Moreover, just as Israel had been the chosen people, so too for Gioberti the Italian people now had an equally special and universal destiny (Sofia 2004). The importance of the Italian exiles' civilising mission was highlighted through an explicit comparison with the exile of the Jews,

»whose migrations, mostly violent and begun well before the Babylonian captivity and the ›dispersion‹, had a benign influence on the religious opinions and in the institutions of many nations, especially the Japetic ones, bringing them the seeds of many legitimate Semitic traditions, unknown or forgotten by them« (Gioberti 1938a, 253).

As had been the case for Mickiewicz, the perfect coincidence between the nationality and the universality of their cultures, justified the role of the Italian exiles as »Apostles« of a superior moral and political message in Europe. What resulted was a peculiar form of universalism, based not on the values of freedom, equality and democracy – as had been the case with Mazzini – but rather on religious affiliations. This is why Gioberti discouraged the Italian exiles from approaching or being seduced by the political cultures they would encounter when abroad. Thus Gioberti wrote in his *Del Primato morale e civile degli italiani*:

»Beware of adopting the customs and errors of the country where you live: indeed, study the men and their affairs; but keep the national genius intact, and keep yourself untainted by foreign opinions and customs: Know yourselves to be freeborn Italians, thinking and feeling in true Italian fashion even among the barbarians, since the best proof you can give of a noble affection for your native land is to resist foreign blandishments [...] Despite the miserable examples of the current century keep faith in Christ, as the most glorious Italian banner. Be good Catholics, without shame and ostentation [...]« (Gioberti 1938b, 203)

And in the *Prolegomeni del Primato* he warned the exiles against foreign cultural influences, employing for the purpose a striking metaphor likening cultural to biological purity:

»Now living far from one's nest condemns a man of generous disposition to an unremitting war against the exotic influences which assail him from all sides, and combine to smother and to alter his very nature, whereas the weak being unequal to the task and supposing themselves vanquished, are swept along by the torrent of foreign things that surround them, and though mediocre before they are now of no account at all. Being able neither to divest themselves of their own nature and to destroy ingrained habits, not to embrace those that are alien to them, they become hybrid and amphibious, lose their productive vein, and resemble those plants which, once transplanted from their climate and native soil, become wholly sterile, or at best produce infertile flowers which do not set, and vengeful fruit which do not ripen, and are as little fitted to perpetuating the species as they are to rewarding the efforts of those who cultivate them.« (Gioberti 1938a, 252)

Catholic universalism thus legitimised a particularly chauvinistic brand of national identity. Gioberti replaced the democratic values underlying Mazzinian patriotism with those of religion. According to Gioberti, emigration had first and foremost to become the main instrument for the advancement of Christian values, so as to confirm the idea of the Roman and Italian primacy that informed his entire work. Both Mazzini and Gioberti alike were doubtless influenced by Mickiewicz's notion of pilgrimage, but their exiles advanced somewhat different ideas of nationality.

Catholic Reactions: True Christian Exile and Patriotism

The production of a patriotic, revolutionary and democratic discourse of exile so profoundly marked and influenced by religious imagery and ideas, did not go unchallenged, however, in nineteenth-century Europe. Since 1789 the transfer of the sacred that had characterised post-revolutionary political culture was in fact perceived as a grave threat by the Church. The penetration of revolutionary politics produced in Italy, as everywhere else in Europe, a violent intellectual reaction. As Luciano Guerci has recently demonstrated for the Italian case, between 1789 and 1799 counterrevolutionary writers saw in the language of the French revolution not only the reversal of their traditional values, but also a devious attempt to impose alternative religions founded on deceit and false premises, heresies that many observers viewed as direct filiations of Jansenism or of the Protestant reform (Guerci 2008). Revolutionary language posed a direct threat to the value system of the Catholic Church. The idea of national sovereignty at the foundation of the *Risorgimento* project, at least in its democratic version, represented the negation of the principle of authority (Traniello 2007, 62).

The spreading of the revolutionary political culture had another consequence: it forced traditional Catholics not only to condemn the new words and principles, but also to argue against them and engage with the underlying ideas. The resulting dialogue between ideological opponents produced a fascinating range of hybrid forms: since what took place was not merely a clash, but also a discursive exchange: national movements may well have borrowed religious ideas and images, but reactionary intellectuals and commentators were likewise often forced to adopt and re-define the revolutionary vocabulary in anti-revolutionary terms. The interpretation of both religious concepts such as martyrdom, sacrifice, apostolate and regeneration, and political ones, such as freedom, patriotism universalism, philanthropy and equality, produced a competition and cultural wars that forced both sides to discuss in a compelling and convincing way their respective definitions and meanings. This intellectual confrontation, inaugurated in the 1790s, continued in the following decades. Like the conservative commentators during the French revolution, the reactionary writers of Restoration Italy, blamed the revolutionary culture for having radically transformed the language of politics, morals and religion, and for cheating public opinion with a vocabulary based on mistaken principles. To prove their case, they produced a number of catechisms and dictionaries presenting their own »correct« definitions. This engagement stemmed from a growing awareness that censorship was no longer a sufficient tool to counter the rise of liberalism and national sentiment, and that an effective cultural and ideological offensive had to be devised to influence public opinion (del Corno 1997, 42–4). Indeed, anti-liberal writers were in principle hostile to any form of education and spreading of literary culture among the popular classes, as they saw in it a direct threat to social hierarchies and to the principle of authority. However, faced with the success of their adversaries, they were forced to change strategy (del Corno 1998).

The Catholic reactions to Lamennais' revolutionary interpretation of the New Testament, and to the patriotic literature influenced by it, represent an interesting case-study of the ideological and discursive battles that took place in the 1830s in Europe. The exceptional success of Lamennais' *Paroles* in Europe account for the wide range of reactions and condemnations produced in the years following its publication.[15] The fact that Lamennais' revolutionary and democratic programme was disguised as a religious and evangelical message made his work even more subversive and destabilising in the eyes of his enemies. For the Catholic convert Karl Ludwig von Haller, Lamennais' ideas represented the work of Satan, and conveyed a deep hatred for God and those who respected him, embodying as it did the same spirit of destruction that had animated the French revolution (von Haller 1835, 7–9).

In responding to Lamennais' *Paroles* and to his Italian imitators, Francesco Borioni's lengthy *Parole di un Patriota Cristiano* [Pesaro, 1834] reflect very many of the concerns and the ideological features of this reactionary literature. Although Borioni admitted that both he and Lamennais had based their writings on Holy Scriptures, the results were »two parts that had an entirely opposite nature« (Borioni 1834, 6). Borioni was at pains to prove that patriotism was by no means exclusively owned by the enemies of the Church. His Christian patriots did not love Italy less than their revolutionary counterparts did. However, Borioni argued, true Italian patriotism demanded first and foremost a love for one's sovereign, as the worthiest of the citizens of one's country. Likewise in his view equality had to be understood as no more than equality before the law and in the enjoyment of social right, since the dependence that each order had on the other represented the foundation of human society (Borioni 1934, 11 and 36). It was God, Borioni argued, who had designed nations and appointed Monarchs. A Christian patriot was such because he respected the political order that God had designed, and also because being a true believer and a member of the Catholic Church, he had embraced the only religion to be genuinely universal (ibid., 26–7). Thus patriotism was both a universal and religious concept, and a narrower, intrinsecally political affiliation. Any other forms of patriotism were doomed to be nothing but forms of anarchism (ibid., 34). Finally Borioni condemned the penetration of foreign cultures and ideas in Italy as a threat to Italian patriotism and culture: »Do not put your trust in those foreigners who deceive you.« (Ibid., 31–2 and 33–4).

Another example of the responses to Lamennais is offered by one of the principal representatives of the reactionary party in Restoration Italy, Monaldo Leopardi (del Corno 1992, 106–125; Meriggi 1992). Leopardi,

15 For a list of reactions see also (Verucci 1963).

whose works sold and were reprinted in thousands of copies, was among the most popular of the anti-*Risorgimento* writers (del Corno 1992, 117). His *Le Parole di un credente, come le scrisse F. De La Mennais quando era un credente* [Modena, 1836] show how Catholic culture could mount a challenge to the democratic and revolutionary reinterpretations of human exile from God. In this pamphlet Leopardi reconciled the theme of exile and patriotism with a traditional and anti-revolutionary social, political and religious vision and reinterpreted the work of Lamennais by claiming to have retrieved the original message of the *Paroles d'un croyant*, the one the French writer himself had advocated before falling victim to the ideas of »a febrile and delirious age« (Leopardi 1836, V). For Leopardi a man is exiled and a wanderer not when oppressed by evil and waiting for Christ to announce freedom in the world, but rather when, as a sinner, he rebels against the laws of God and against obedience to his legitimate sovereign. The individualism, popular sovereignty and equality defended by Lamennais represented a direct challenge to his organic vision of society, and a threat to the divine order. Rejecting the revolutionary interpretation of the Gospel, for Leopardi it was humankind's rebellion against God's will and against the natural social and political order he had designed, not social injustices, that had condemned it to eternal exile. Only a blind obedience could put an end to human exile from God:

»You see him wandering and alone on the earth! May God save that wretch that has been led astray! I walked amongst the peoples; they looked at me; I looked at them, and we did not recognise each other. Everybody is a stranger to the rebel and the enemy of God.« (Leopardi 1836, 151)

During his journey on earth, man had to reject the lures of the enemies of religion, that is to say those who advocated the »spreading of enlightenment«, and flooded »the Earth with irreligious and false books« (ibid., 42). In Leopardi's view salvation, possible only with the compliance of God's laws, could only be granted after death. Thus, against Lamennais, he confined redemption to its traditional transcendental dimension:

»You have neither land nor homeland: the rebel is the exile from all homelands. Poor wretch and stray! In vain you hasten to look for a homeland. Man's homeland is Heaven, and there is no homeland for the enemy of Heaven. He goes wandering about the earth, and cannot find a homeland on earth, may God save that wretch who has been led astray!« (Ibid. 152–3)

Against the views of the Italian nationalists, Leopardi adopted both a Christian and a transcendental interpretation of *patria*, (Heaven being the only true homeland to humankind), and one that was anti-national from a political perspective. For Leopardi the homeland was in fact first and foremost one's city, or at most the borders of one's country of origin. Thus he rejected the political meaning of Italian nation advanced by the Italian revolutionaries, and denounced its fictitious nature, based as it was on the imagination of a community that in reality did not exist.[16] The revolutionaries in fact wanted to breach »those natural barriers that divide a people from another«, and deprive »each particular people of their usages and national customs« (Leopardi 1836, 43). Between the attachment to one's town and catholic universalism there was no space for the crucial role as intermediary Mazzini or Gioberti had attributed to the nations in reconciling individuals and humanity. To Leopardi human exile thus represented metaphorically an alienation and a punishment due to the rebellion against a natural order that was at the same time divine and earthly, of which the *Risorgimento* represented an intolerable subversion.

Conclusions

The patriots' descriptions of the exiles demonstrate the strategic importance attributed to emigration in implementing revolutionary political programmes. Mazzini, Mickiewicz and Gioberti alike thought it to be of vital importance to ensure the support of the exile communities, as without their contribution any ideological or political battle would have been unsuccessful. It is not by chance that many, if not all of the most important texts of the Italian *Risorgimento*, from the Manifesto of »Young Italy« to the works of Gioberti and Tommaseo, were addressed to the exiles, or included sections or chapters explicitly devoted to instructing and educating the exiles. Their goal was to maintain the political mobilisation of the patriots abroad, and at the same time to offer convincing rhetorical instruments capable of investing the mass experience of emigration with a meaning. From this point of view the images and narrative devices discussed above had an eminently political function, complementing the struggles

16 See his Catechismo filosofico per uso delle scuole inferiori proposto dai redattori della »Voce della ragione« [Pesaro, 1832], now in (Del Corno 1992, 146–155).

and the plots of those years. The descriptions advanced by the Italian patriots in the wake of Lamennais and Mickiewicz became powerful tools of patriotic propaganda that maintained their efficacy well beyond the end of the *Risorgimento*, as they contributed to the construction of a national memory of the period. Perhaps the most telling example is provided by Mazzini's re-utilisation of the representation of the young exiles first published in 1834 in his *Autobiographical Memoirs*, whereby his description of triumphant youth ineluctably destined to win its battle for the principle of nationality in Europe became an element of the representation of the *Risorgimento* after 1860. The effectiveness of these images lay in their ability to transform what was arguably a condition of marginality, distance, exclusion and defeat – since exile was for most of the patriots the consequence of political failure, to which many others were to come – , into an eminently ethical choice, into a mission not only useful but also necessary, as it was linked to the unavoidable and inescapable accomplishment of freedom and national independence, as elements of an divine design to be fulfilled in history. What I have tried to demonstrate is the existence of a discourse of exile in which the exiles became the vanguard of the nation. From being powerless victims of history, they were turned into its primary protagonists and agents. Whereas the martyrs' duty was to bear witness to the faith in the patriotic cause with their death, the pilgrims, apostles and the exiles from God's homeland had to preach its principles across the world and make its inevitable victory possible.

At the same time, however, the metaphors drawn from religious language were adopted by patriots who had different ideological programmes. While it may hardly be surprising that these re-appropriations encountered fierce resistance from reactionary Catholic culture, which strove to reinsert them within the framework of traditional theology, it is worth highlighting how a patriotic discourse of exile could advance and help to disseminate ideas of nation and universality that had little in common with one another. There is no doubt that both Mazzini and Gioberti shared a common hostility to the French revolutionary tradition. However, Mazzini's critique presupposed an understanding of democracy that was indebted to the revolution itself. Moreover, the exiles' mission, as understood by Mazzini and by Gioberti respectively, aimed at almost diverging patriotisms and universalisms. For Mazzini, the mission of the exiles of the European nations mutually allied was that of ensuring the triumph of democracy and equality, according to a principle of nationality in which the political and voluntaristic dimension prevailed over the cultural (Urbinati 2008).[17] In Gioberti, by contrast, the idea of the nation was based on the primacy of the Italian and Catholic culture, whose universal values were superior to any other cultural model that might be encountered abroad. What issued from the exilic discourse advanced by Gioberti, as well as by Mickiewicz, was a profound intolerance towards other cultures and a pre-eminence of religious values in the definition of nation and civilisation that we cannot find in Mazzini's works. To borrow Michel Winock's definition, Lamennais, Mazzini and their imitators stood for an »open« nationalism, generous towards the other nationalities, based on the defence of the oppressed and on notions of democracy; while Mickiewicz and Gioberti represented a »closed« brand of nationalism that, in spite of an attachment to the principles of European brotherhood, advanced a somewhat xenophobic and culturally narrow definition of the nation, based on the idea of a superior religion, intolerant of other cultural models and foreign ideas (Wincock 1990, 11–40, and esp. 37–40). From this point of view, Gioberti and Mickiewicz were closer to the Catholic reactionaries like Francesco Borioni, who warned against the imitation of foreigners in order to protect patriotism, than to Mazzini or Lamennais. Thus, an analysis of the religious influences on the debates about patriotism and exile challenges any simplistic dichotomy between national movements and their ideological enemies, and demonstrates not only the internal fissures or divisions within patriotic languages, but also the existence of a measure of continuity and common ground between reactionary-anti-national and national discourses.

Works cited

Aniello, Tommaso (1836). *L'Inno all'esule.* Turin: C.A. Carignano.

Anon. (1848). *L'esule e la sua patria.* Locarno: no publisher.

Banti, Alberto M. (2000). *La nazione del Risorgimento. Parentela, santità e onore alle origini dell'Italia unita.* Turin: Einaudi.

Banti, Alberto M. (2008). Sacrality and the Aesthetics of Politics: Mazzini's Concept of the Nation. In Christopher A. Bayly and Eugenio F. Biagini (eds.). *Giuseppe Mazzini and the Globalisation of Democratic Nationalism 1830–1920*, 59–74. Oxford, New York: Oxford University Press for The British Academy.

17 For a different interpretation of Mazzini's idea of nationhood, which highlights its natural and metaphoric dimension as a cultural contract see (Banti 2008, 59–74).

Biagini, Eugenio F. (2008). Mazzini and Anticlericalism: The English Exile. In Christopher A. Bayly and Eugenio F. Biagini (eds.). *Giuseppe Mazzini and the Globalisation of Democratic Nationalism 1830–1920*, 145–166. Oxford, New York: Oxford University Press for The British Academy.

Bitton-Ashkelony, Brouria (2005). *Encountering the sacred: the debate on Christian Pilgrimage*. Berkeley: University of California Press.

Bonsanti, Marta (2007). Amore familiare, amore romantico e amor di patria. In Alberto M. Banti and Paul Ginsborg (eds.). *Il Risorgimento*, 128–152. Turin: Einaudi.

Borioni, Francesco (1834). *Parole di un Patriota Cristiano*. Pesaro: Nobili.

Del Corno, Nicola (1992). *Gli scritti sani. Dottrina e propaganda della reazione italiana dalla Restaurazione all'unità*. Milano: F. Angeli.

Del Corno, Nicola (1997). *La formazione dell'opinione pubblica e la libertà di stampa nella pubblicistica reazionaria del Risorgimento (1831–1847)*. Florence: Le Monnier.

Del Corno, Nicola (1998). »L'abuso dei lumi«. I reazionari e il problema dell'educazione nell'Italia del Risorgimento. *Società e Storia*, 21, 799–830.

Eade, John, and Michael J. Sallnow (2000). *Contesting the Sacred: the anthropology of Christian pilgrimage*. Urbana: University of Illinois Press.

Evans, Craig A. (1997). Aspects of Exile and Restoration in the Proclamation of Jesus and the Gospels. In James M. Scott (ed.). *Exile, Old Testament, Jewish and Christian Conceptions*, 299–328. Leiden, New York: Brill.

Francia, Enrico (2007). »Il nuovo Cesare è la patria«. Clero e religione nel lungo Quarantotto italiano. In Alberto M. Banti and Paul Ginsborg (eds.). *Il Risorgimento*, 423–450. Turin: Einaudi.

Freitag, Sabine (ed.). (2003). *Exiles from European Revolutions. Refugees in Mid-Victorian England*. New York: Berghahn Books.

Gentile, Emilio (1996). *The Sacralization of Politics in fascist Italy*. Cambridge/Mass.: Harvard University Press.

Gentile, Emilio (2001). *Le religioni della politica. Fra democrazie e totalitarismi*. Rome: Laterza.

Ginsborg, Paul (2007). Romanticismo e Risorgimento: l'io, l'amore e la nazione. In Alberto M. Banti and Paul Ginsborg (eds.). *Il Risorgimento*, 5–67. Turin: Einaudi.

Gioberti, Vincenzo (1938a). *Prolegomeni del Primato morale e civile degli italiani*. Ed. Enrico Castelli. Milan: Fratelli Bocca (Edizione Nazionale delle opere edite e inedite di Vincenzo Gioberti).

Gioberti, Vincenzo (1938b). *Del Primato morale e civile degli italiani*. Ed. Ugo Redano. Milan: Fratelli Bocca (Edizione Nazionale delle opere edite e inedite di Vincenzo Gioberti).

Guerci, Luciano (2008). *Uno spettacolo non mai più veduto nel mondo. La rivoluzione francese come unicità e rovesciamento negli scrittori controrivoluzionari italiani (1789–1799)*. Turin: UTET libreria.

Haller, Karl Ludwig von(1835). *Satansso e la Rivoluzione contrapposto alle Parole d'un credente [of Lamennais]*. Modena: Tipografia Camerale.

Hunt, Lynn (1984). *Politics, Culture, and Class in the French Revolution*. Berkeley: University of California Press.

Isabella, Maurizio, (2006) Exile and Nationalism: the Case of the Risorgimento, *European History Quarterly*, 36, 493–520.

Isabella, Maurizio (2008). Mazzini's Internationalism in Context: From the Cosmopolitan Patriotism of the Italian Carbonari to Mazzini's Europe of the Nations, in Christopher A. Bayly and Eugenio F. Biagini (eds.), *Giuseppe Mazzini and the Globalisation of Democratic Nationalism 1820–1920*, 37–58. Oxford, New York: Oxford University press for the British Academy.

Jaume, Lucien (1997). *L'individu effacé, ou le paradoxe du libéralisme français*. Paris: Fayard.

Koropeckyj, Roman (2001). *The Poetics of Revitalization. Adam Mickiewicz Between Forefathers' Eve, part 3, and Pan Tadeusz*. New York: Columbia University Press.

Kramer, Lloyd S. (1988). *Threshold of a New World. Intellectuals and the Exile Experience in Paris, 1830–1848*. Ithaca: Cornell University Press.

Lambert, Frédéric. (2001). *Théologie de la République. Lamennais, prophéte et législateur.* Paris: L'Harmattan.

Lamennais, Félicité. (1891). *Words of a Believer and the Past and Future of the People.* London: Chapman and Hall.

Leopardi, Monaldo (1836). *Le Parole di un credente, come le scrisse F. De La Mennais quando era un credente*. Modena: G. Vicenzi.

Levis Sullam, Simon (ed.). (2004a). Risorgimento italiano e religioni politiche. *Società e Storia*, 27 (special issue).

Levis Sullam, Simon (2004b). »Fate della rivoluzione una religione«: aspetti del nazionalismo mazziniano come religione politica (1831–1835). In Simon Levis Sullam (ed.). Risorgimento italiano e religioni politiche. *Società e Storia*, 27, 705–730.

Mazzini, Giuseppe. (1891). »Lamennais«. In Robert de Lamennais and Hugues Félicité. *Words of a Believer and the Past and Future of the People*, 23. Transl. by L.E. Martineau. London: Chapman and Hall.

Mazzini, Giuseppe (1908a). *Scritti Editi e Inediti*, IV. Imola: Galeati.

Mazzini, Giuseppe (1908b). Ils sont partis. In Giuseppe Mazzini. *Scritti Editi ed Inediti*, 97–100. Imola: Galeati.

Mazzini, Giuseppe (1944). *Note Autobiografiche*. Ed. by M. Menghini, second edition. Florence: F. le Monnier.

Menozzi, Daniele (1986). Tra riforma e restaurazione. Dalla crisi della società cristiana al mito della cristianità medievale (1758–1848). In Giorgio Chittolini and Giovanni Miccoli (eds.). *La Chiesa e il potere politico dal Medioevo all'età contemporanea*, 769–806. Turin: Einaudi.

Meriggi, Marco (1992). Monaldo Leopardi cattolico radicale. *Proposte e Ricerche*, 21, 39–54.

Mickiewicz, Adam (1833). *Livre des Pélérins Polonais, traduit du Polonais d'A.M. par le Comte C. de Montalembert, suivi d'un hymne à la Pologne par F. de Lamennais*. Paris: no publisher.

Mickiewicz, Adam (1944). The Books of the Polish Nation and of the Polish Pilgrims. In George R. Noyes (ed.). *Poems by Adam Mickiewicz*. New York: Polish Institute of Arts and Sciences in America.

Modena, Gustavo (1957). Epistola di Lando ai giovani italiani [Paris, 1835]. In Terenzio Grandi (ed.). *Scritti e Discorsi di Gustavo Modena (1831–1860)*, 58–72. Rome: Istituto per la storia del Risorgimento italiano.

Riall, Lucy (2008). »I martiri nostri son tutti risorti!«. Garibaldi, i garibaldini e il culto della morte eroica nel Risorgimento. In Oliver Janz and Lutz Klinkhammer (eds.). *La morte per la patria. La celebrazione dei caduti dal Risorgimento alla Repubblica*, 23–44. Rome: Donzelli.

Romani, Roberto (2006). L'economia politica dei moderati 1830–48. *Società e Storia*, 29, 21–50.

Roppen, George and Richard Sommer (1964), *Strangers and Pilgrims: An Essay on the Metaphor of Journey*. Oslo: Humanities Press.

Sancipriano, Mario (1973). *Lamennais in Italia. Autorità e libertà nel pensiero filosofico-religioso del Risorgimento*. Milan: Marzorati.

Sarti, Roland (1997). *Mazzini. A life for the Religion of Politics*. Westport, Connecticut: Praeger.

Sarti, Roland (2008). Giuseppe Mazzini and Young Europe. In Christopher A. Bayly and Eugenio F. Biagini (eds.), *Giuseppe Mazzini and the Globalisation of Democratic Nationalism 1830–1920*, 275–297. Oxford, New York: Oxford University Press for The British Academy.

Scott, James M. (ed.). (1997). *Exile, Old Testament, Jewish and Christian Conceptions*. Leiden, New York: Brill.

Sofia, Francesca (2001): Ebrei e Risorgimento: Appunti per una ricerca. In Gian Paolo Romagnani (ed.). *La Bibbia, La Coccarda e il tricolore. I valdesi fra due Emancipazioni (1798–1848)*, 349–367. Turin: Claudiana.

Sofia, Francesca (2004). Le fonti bibliche nel Primato Italiano di Vincenzo Gioberti. *Società e Storia*, 27, 747–762.

Talmon, Jacob Laib (1960). *Political Messianism. The Romantic Phase*. London: Praeger.

Tilysinska, Anna (2004). La religione della patria in Mickiewicz e Towianski: influenze polacche sul Risorgimento italiano. *Società e Storia*, 106, 763–779.

Traniello, Francesco (1992). Religione, nazione e sovranità nel Risorgimento italiano. *Rivista di Storia e Letteratura Religiosa*, 28, 319–68.

Traniello, Francesco (2007). *Religione cattolica e Stato nazionale. Dal Risorgimento al secondo dopoguerra*. Bologna: Il mulino.

Turner, Victor and Edith (1978). *Image and Pilgrimage in Christian Culture: Anthropological Perspectives*. New York: Columbia University Press.

Urbinati, Nadia (2008). The Legacy of Kant: Giuseppe Mazzini's Cosmopolitanism of Nations. In Christopher A. Bayly and Eugenio F. Biagini (eds.). *Giuseppe Mazzini and the Globalisation of Democratic Nationalism*, 11–35. Oxford, New York: Oxford University Press for The British Academy.

Varouxakis, Giorgios (2006, 5). Introduction: Patriotism and Nationhood in Nineteenth-Century European Political Thought. *European Journal of Political Theory*, 5/1, 7–11.

Verucci, G. (1963). *Félicité Lamennais. Dal cattolicesimo autoritario al radicalismo democratico.* Naples: Nella sede dell'Istituto.

Winock, Michel (1990). *Nationalisme, antisémitisme et fascisme en France.* Paris: Seuil.

Nationalism and Anti-Cosmopolitanism in the Russian Radical Right and Soviet Ideology

Frank Grüner

»In Soviet Russia, ›cosmopolitan‹ is a dirty word, and it is once again increasingly applied to the Soviet Union's 3,000,000 Jews.« (Anti-Cosmopolitanism 1961)

This is what was written in an article in the *Time* magazine, dated 24 November 1961. It concerned the phenomenon of anti-cosmopolitanism in the Soviet Union. On examination of the official and semi-official discourses of the nineteenth and twentieth centuries it becomes evident that the concept of a cosmopolitan and of »cosmopolitanism« has in general never been understood as something genuinely positive in Russia. This applies to Russia under the tsars, as well as during the Soviet and post-Soviet periods. At first glance it is hard to imagine why the idea of »cosmopolitanism«, which in itself is strongly linked with tolerance and humanitarian ideals, and which requires surmounting national, ethical or racist limitations, could, in the Russian context, meet with such unanimous rejection. This negative attitude is even more surprising when we consider that, in the case of Russia and in the time period relevant for this research, we are after all dealing with three different state structures, which, in terms of their political system and their official ideology, are vastly dissimilar regimes: the autocratic regime before 1917, the Soviet regime between 1917 and 1991, and finally the semi-democratic Russia under presidents Yeltsin and Putin.

In Russia not only is a predominantly negative reception of the concept of »cosmopolitanism« apparent, but also one sees the existence of an ideology of »anti-cosmopolitanism«.

The possible origins of this ideology of »anti-cosmopolitanism« will be discussed in the following passages. The precise aim of this article is to highlight the existence and function of »anti-cosmopolitanism« in the ideology of the Russian Right before 1917 and in the ideological and political basis of the late Stalinist era, and to compare them. On the basis of this comparison the central question of the extent to which the ideology of

»anti-cosmopolitanism« can be understood as a feature of modern Russian nationalism and chauvinism respectively shall be pursued. First of all, however, I would like to make a few brief comments about the history of the word or the concept of »cosmopolitanism« in the Russian context.

The idea of »cosmopolitanism« in the Russian context

It is not clear when exactly the concepts of »the cosmopolitan« and of »cosmopolitanism« itself first entered the Russian language. Their common usage since the middle of the nineteenth century can certainly be verified. One of the earliest examples for a description of a »cosmopolitan« in Russian literature dates from 1850s. The famous Russian writer Ivan Goncharov described in his popular travel novel Fregat Pallada (first published in 1858) a typical »cosmopolitan« in the following way:

»Pale face, fair hair, profile [...] a Jewish profile exactly. No doubt. However, in spite of this guess, some of us were still sceptical, questioning this opinion. Indeed, nothing about him was English: he does not look with his eyes wide open; his thought, reasoning, is not wedged in some kind of vise like an Englishman; he does not sift one word at the time, awkwardly, through his teeth. With this fellow thoughts flow so playfully and freely: obviously, his mind is not oppressed by prejudices; his views do not fit into the English cut, like a starched necktie. Well, in a word, everything was as it could be only with a cosmopolitan, that is, a kike.« (Goncharov 1899, 5: 188–9. Cited in Weiner 2001, 196)

Obviously already in that time the concepts »cosmopolitan« and »kike« (Russian *zhid*, pejorative appellation for »Jew«) had a largely similar meaning in Russia. This is true in particular since 1881/1882, when Tsar Alexander II was murdered and the widespread wave of anti-Jewish pogroms in the Russian Empire took place (Haberer 1992, 98–134). Later they were most notably used in the time subsequent to the proclamation of the October Manifest of 1905, once again a phase of political agitation and of extreme violence in Russia, primarily against Jews. As for the conservative Goncharov, considerable parts of Russian society, especially within the nationalist and reactionary elites, viewed all developments of political, economic or social change inside Russia with deep mistrust. The Jews in particular were considered as agents of modernisation and change. This was true to some extent not least because of the extraordinary social structure of the Jewish population in the Tsarist Empire (Löwe 1978, e.g. 11–3, 17–39, 199–207). But beyond this reality, Jews were frequently regarded as agents of modern capitalism and as representatives of a revolutionary socialism at the same time. These anti-Jewish stereotypes had an important influence on the formation of a modern anti-Semitism in Russia (ibid., 11–3, 17–29, 106–45, 199–207). In Russian conservative and reactionary thinking these negative images of the Jews were somehow linked to the widespread understanding of the »pernicious work« of cosmopolitans within Russian society. And in spite of all inner inconsistencies one can find a sort of »cosmopolitan-anti-Semitic paradigm« in Russian nationalistic ideology, as Erich Haberer called it (Haberer 1992, 100).

In his esteemed *Explanatory dictionary of the living Great Russian language* of 1881 linguist Vladimir Dahl describes a »cosmopolitan« relatively neutrally as a »citizen of the world« (Weltbürger) and a »non-resident«, as well as »a person who does not recognize any particular ties to his homeland« (Dal' 1881, 173)

The renowned Russian-language encyclopaedia Brokgauz and Efron of 1895 likewise characterises the terms »cosmopolitanism« and »cosmopolitan« initially in view of their roots in antique philosophy and their further conceptual development as fundamentally positive ideas, which in the awareness of mankind's unity strives for the surmounting of individual interests of the separate states and peoples in favour of the common good of mankind as a whole (Brokgauz and Efron 1895, 378–9).

Cosmopolitanism, however, is in the process very often interpreted »only in a negative sense, as the simple absence of patriotism or love towards one's own people and fatherland« (ibid., 379). Brokgauz and Efron make it unmistakably clear that this sort of perception, whereby the struggle for the interests of mankind and love for the fatherland are mutually exclusive, is by no means correct (ibid., 379). Evidently, in their criticism of the one-sided negative perception of the phenomenon of »cosmopolitanism«, the authors were in addition or above all mindful of the Russian-nationalistic discourses of the eighties and nineties of the nineteenth century.

Against the background of the political conflicts of that time, however, in particular since the Russian Revolution of 1905, the idea of »cosmopolitanism« was already interpreted in a solely negative way by the Russian press, above all in the organs of the Russian Radical Right (Rogger 1986, 191). Thus, the nationalistic, »patriotic« press attacked their political opponents, who consisted of all revolutionaries and enemies of autocracy respectively, as »Jews«, »freemasons«, »socialists« and »liberals«, or in fact sweepingly as »cosmopolitans« and »cosmopolitan intelligentsia«. After the Russian parliament, known as the Duma, had been seized from the Tsar by the revolutionary movement in 1905, it was defamed by the far-right reactionary forces as a »cosmopolitan« institution »undercut by Jews«. Even with regards to foreign affairs, everything that was classed as »alien« and »hostile« was automatically branded »Jewish« and »cosmopolitan«, and was therefore vilified from the point of view of the Russian Radical Right.

A wide range of examples shows that in the last years of the tsarist period the concept of a »cosmopolitan« was largely, if not exclusively, used as a synonym for the word »Jew«. In all of these cases »cosmopolitan« and »cosmopolitanism« clearly have negative connotations. However, it was not the traditional, orthodox Jews living in the *schtetls* of the Russian Empire who were referred to as »cosmopolitans«, but rather the members of the new secularised, russified intelligentsia in the cities of the tsardom. The autocratic regime and the conservative and far right forces of Russian society encountered this new, »modern« class of generally well-educated and often successful russified Jews with deep mistrust and on occasion referred to them contemptuously as »Jewish rationalists, venal and faceless cosmopolitans« (Löwe 1993, 47). The emergence and dynamic growth of the revolutionary movement, in which the Jews were disproportionately well-represented, relative to their share of the population, further strengthened the general tendency to group together cosmopolitans, Jews, revolutionaries, socialists and liberals, in particular within the far right camp.

Even the originally positive meaning in terms of a liberal-minded person or »citizen of the world« experienced an unmistakably negative transformation in the Russian interpretation of the word »cosmopolitan«. Jews and »cosmopolitans« not only tried to undermine the existing order from within, but also worked in conjunction with Russia's foreign enemies to plot her destruction. In this context the idea of a worldwide Jewish conspiracy, as was expressed for instance in the *Protocols of the Elders of Zion*, achieved a disastrous effect. Allegedly the Jews not only exerted control over world capital and the world press, but were also striving towards world domination.

In line with the anti-Semitic outlook and the aggressive propaganda of the extreme right, »Jews« and »cosmopolitans« ultimately became generic terms for all conceptualisations of the political enemy, as well as a discursive weapon against particularly despised groups in Russian society. In this way the extreme right, with their overtly schematic political ideology, portrayed the Jews and cosmopolitans in contrast to that of the idealised »true Russians« who were of course »loyal to the tsar«, »orthodox« and patriotic.

The negatively charged term »cosmopolitanism«, as presented here, was especially prevalent in the conservative and reactionary elements of pre-revolutionary Russia. In contrast to, or in an extension of, this concept, Jeffrey Brooks has tried to demonstrate that there had also been a degree of openness in parts of Russian society to the foreign and cosmopolitan dating back to the mid-nineteenth century, as demonstrated in the appropriation of certain ideas, lifestyles and social and economic practices:

»Reform, Glasnost, and a cosmopolitan public sensibility comprise a triptych in modern Russian history. Reform obviously hinged on a certain openness in public life, but the link to cosmopolitanism, in the sense of a sympathetic orientation toward foreigners and life abroad, was also powerful. From the 1850s to 1992, reform depended on increased interchange with the other nations and the receptiveness to the surrounding world. Reformers looked to foreign models, foreign opinions were heard in public life, and there was a tendency to accommodate international practice in fields from banking to human rights.« (Brooks 1992, 1431; For that see also Brooks 1985, 226–39)

Despite the accuracy of this claim, the question remains whether a positively defined concept of »cosmopolitanism« could have been established in Russia in parallel to the negatively conceptualised term. Also worthy of consideration is the degree to which foreign ideas, practices and other phenomena, which are »foreign« in the sense of having originated in other countries and cultures, can be interpreted as an expression of a cosmopolitan orientation.

The Idea of »Anti-Cosmopolitanism« in the Ideology of the Russian Radical Right in Pre-Revolutionary Russia

It has become evident that the use of »cosmopolitan« and »cosmopolitanism« in the late tsardom was essentially influenced by anti-Jewish or – more accurately – anti-Semitic sentiments.

In fact, the political thinking of the Russian Radical Right in pre-revolutionary Russia was governed, alongside the perception of a traditional

Russian nationalism, by an anti-Semitic ideology adverse to modernisation. If, at first, traditional values such as orthodoxy, autocracy and the Russian national principle (*narodnost'*) represented the foundations of this philosophy, there emerged towards the end of the nineteenth century an ideological construct, epitomised by the notion »reactionary utopia« (Heinz-Dietrich Löwe), conceptualised in order to oppose the socio-economic and political changes in Russian society (Löwe 1978, 17–29).

The Russian Radical Right shared the idea that the Jews would play a central role in the advancement towards a capitalist society, as well as to parliamentary order. The preconception that the revolution could be defeated and the »true« Russia be preserved through violently fighting back at or striking down the Jews was expressed drastically in numerous Jewish pogroms, following the declaration of the October-Manifesto in 1905. It is precisely against this background that the central slogan of the Russian Radical Right and of the *pogromshchiki*, »Beat the Jews, save Russia!« is to be understood.

Consistent with their counterrevolutionary, reactionary views, »Union of the Russian People« (*Soiuz Russkogo Naroda*), an important group of the radical right that was founded in 1905, as well as the less known, more élite »Union of the Russian Men« (*Soiuz Russkikh Liudei*), interpreted the policy of Sergey Witte, who was serving as Russia's Finance Minister and Prime Minister, as an attempt to submit Russia to the rule of international finance and the market and effectively to dispossess the Russian peasants and gentry (Löwe 1978, 123–125; Rogger 1986, 200–20). The reactionary forces considered the despised bureaucracy to be their primary adversary (Löwe 1978, 123). These bureaucrats, they supposed, were driving themselves between the ruling Tsar and the needs of his subjects. Throughout these transformations, followers of the radical right saw the pernicious influence of Jews and cosmopolitans in all spheres of Russian life, from the highest to the lowest, in operation: »This demagogic combination of anti-bureaucratic, anti-cosmopolitan, anti-urban, anti-Semitic, and anti-capitalist notes [...] was a novelty on the Russian political scene.« (Rogger 1986, 201)

With regard to the conception of the Russian Right as the enemy, which had existed primarily since the Revolution of 1905, one could also allude to an ideology of »anti-cosmopolitanism«. While the Russian Right viewed itself as a defender of the »true« interests of the Russian people and as the preserver of »Russian national character« and of autocracy, it saw in the economic changes, as well as in the constitutional or revolutionary ambitions of its time the destructive force of Jews, freemasons and members of the *intelligentsia*, which it fought decisively, characterising its adversaries as »rootless cosmopolitans«.

It would seem that Russian nationalism of the late nineteenth and early twentieth century needed an anti-cosmopolitan element of this kind, in order to offer an explanation for the fundamental upheavals in Russian society since 1861 and to account for inner political conflicts. In an increasingly developing and changing world, the fight against the hostile principle of cosmopolitanism, covering all areas of everyday life, served, at least amongst the Russian Radical Right, as the central unifying factor for the widely differing views and interests of various groups of the Russian population. Where original principles or values of Russian nationalism no longer sufficed to mobilise large sections of the population into supporting the Tsar and autocracy, an ideological construct was needed as a strategy for integration (Löwe 1978, 121–34). It was precisely this construct that was provided by anti-cosmopolitanism, which could be characterised in essence as a combination of anti-modernisation, anti-Western ideology, brandishing an anti-Semitic conspiracy theory.

A combination of various factors, of which only the most important can be mentioned here, ultimately played a part in the perception and enduring impression of Jews as cosmopolitans:

1. As a non-Russian (*inorodtsy*), non orthodox-Christian minority the Jews remained foreign elements in the eyes of the Slavic-orthodox population, which made up the Russian nation; against the background of the cautious softening of anti-Jewish legislature in the Russian Empire and the struggle for emancipation by parts of Jewish society, in the second half of the nineteenth century, an increasing number of Russians perceived this »foreignness« or »distinctness« of the Jews as a threat to Russian society.
2. The commonly assumed disloyalty of the Jews towards the Tsar and towards autocracy placed them outside the national and patriotic consensus of the majority population.
3. Modern day anti-Semitism was able to draw upon the century long existence of old anti-Jewish prejudices and resentments and therefore maintained a considerable potential to mobilise the population.

»Anti-cosmopolitanism« and anti-Zionism in Soviet ideology

Although anti-Semitism did not, as falsely predicted by the Marxist-Leninist theorists, disappear from society after the revolution of 1917, it at least played no role in the Bolshevik ideology of the 1920s and 1930s. In the wake of the Second World War however, Stalin utilised – most likely deliberately – the anti-Semitism of the Russian Radical Right pre-1917 and its view of Jews as »rootless cosmopolitans without a fatherland« (Grüner 2008, 437–51).

As has already been observed, prior to the October Revolution of 1917, and in particular during the Russia-Japan War (1904/05) and the revolution of 1905 attacks against »cosmopolitans« within the country increased significantly in times of political crisis and especially in times of war. This was also the case during the Second World War and the difficult post-war years. In 1945, an article on »About patriotism« (*O patriotizme*) appeared in the Soviet press, in which the Author N. Baltiiskii discussed in detail »cosmopolitanism« as an ideology foreign to the workers:

»The enemies of the workers regularly attempt also to dispute the patriotism of communist and socialist supporters by referring to their position of international solidarity of the workers. This position is portrayed by our opponents as cosmopolitanism, as an indifferent and contemptible attitude towards the fatherland.

That is quite simply outright slander. Communism has nothing in common with cosmopolitanism. The communist movement of every country as a leading movement of the workers stands firmly on home soil, fighting under the banner of international solidarity. Communism does not bring genuine patriotism into conflict with proletarian internationalism, but connects them both. [...]

Moreover, precisely because of their indefatigable pursuit of the Golden Calf, international speculators not only willingly sell, they also readily sell themselves to foreign imperialists who offer the highest price. Not only in neutral states have they proven in great number to be financial cosmopolitans, but they have also shown themselves to be willing accomplices of the German-fascist aggressor in France and in Anglo-Saxon countries. [...]

It has thus been established that the cosmopolitanism of the international monopolists and speculators is not the least bit ›non-political‹. «. (Baltiiskii 1945, 3–11.)

The large extent to which the Stalinist regime distanced itself in its media from all personal connections to cosmopolitanism as a »deeply unpatriotic ideology« is certainly striking. The epithets, synonyms or appellations which are attributed in this article to the hated »cosmopolitans«, e.g. (scrupulous) »profiteers«, »international speculators«, »financial cosmopolitans«,

»dealers of death« or »accomplices of the German-fascist aggressor« resemble, nearly word-for-word, the predominantly anti-Jewish but also anti-liberal, anti-democratic and anti-cosmopolitan concepts of the Russian Right during the last two to three decades leading up to the Revolution of 1917. In this article of 1945 the *Novoe vremja* still see »cosmopolitans« first and foremost as belonging to the enemies of the Soviet people, as well as being members of the »neutral states«. The »cosmopolitans« within the homeland are not yet explicitly named here, but without a doubt it was part of the inner logic of the Stalinist system that there must also be »internal« enemies, agents or allies of the Soviet state's »external« enemies.

In the politics of the so-called *Zhdanovshchina*, which was heralded with the party decrees of August 1946 and an aggressive campaign in the press, a new era of Soviet patriotism was carved out, in which the Russian-nationalistic element was taken to absurdity; at the start of the Cold War the aim was to break away from the »bourgeois-decadent« West and to triumph over it (Grüner 2008, 438–43; Hahn 1982). With the exceptionally stereotyped and at that time thoroughly overblown accusation of the »grovelling nature of the present bourgeois culture of the West«, the regime campaigned against »foreign« and »un-Soviet« ideas in the ranks of the intelligentsia. In the early Cold War period the population was to be isolated from the enemy camp by means of ideology, and at the same time convinced of the superiority of the Soviet system. In order to cope with this task, the intelligentsia itself had, according to the logic of the Soviet system, to be cleansed of all »harmful Western influences«. This objective was strengthened further by a fear bordering on paranoia in the ranks of Soviet leadership of the omnipresence of »subversive elements«, which were suspected to exist not least within the intelligentsia. After the war this deep distrust on the part of the Soviet leadership towards their own people, to which in particular the measures against the intelligentsia after 1946 testify, became a decisive factor in the politics of the Soviet leadership. It is on these foundations that the campaigns against »rootless cosmopolitanism« and Zionism from 1948 onwards, which can only be briefly outlined here, should be viewed.

From the beginning of 1948 leading Soviet newspapers and journals reported in dozens of articles about the »uncovering« of subversive activities of »rootless cosmopolitans« in the entire country. The trigger for the purges, by this time being adopted throughout the country, was the »exposure« of an »anti-patriotic group of theatre critics« in January 1949. The decision to carry out these purges was taken by leading Soviet politicians at a meeting of the central committee on 24 January 1949 with Malenkov presiding, and was most likely initiated by Stalin himself. The criticism was already present in the forefront of the campaigns alongside the »anti-patriotic« and »bourgeois-esthetic« orientation of a group of theatre critics, above all as a result of the »national formation« of Soviet critics overall. During these months, in various regions of the Soviet Union, hundreds of Soviet intellectuals, mostly of Jewish origin, were removed from their posts in all areas of culture, science, economy and administration. Often, they were imprisoned. Extensive purges were carried out in publishing houses and newspapers, in cultural societies, in orchestras, opera houses, theatres, in the film industry, in museums, at universities, institutes of higher education, academies of music, research institutes and other academic and cultural facilities, in hospitals and clinics, in ministries, at the higher levels of bureaucracy, and in various state and party organs (Grüner 2008, 443–51; Kostyrchenko 2001, 310–50).

The campaigns against the »rootless cosmopolitans« took place in an extremely tense and frequently hysterical atmosphere, which resulted above all from the existential insecurity of all those involved, but also from the frosty environment of the general political climate. Although the repressions associated with the campaigns were not exclusively aimed at Jews, they nevertheless had a most significant effect on representatives of the Jewish intelligentsia. Simply because of their origins, Jews were equated with »cosmopolitans« and »Zionists«, despite the fact that everyone could fundamentally be subjected to the same »accusations«. Amir Weiner also encapsulates this anti-Jewish bias of the Stalinist regime's anti-cosmopolitan ideology when he writes:

»The core message of the anticosmopolitan campaign in the late 1940s was that the Jew remained a Jew, an eternal alien to the national body, despite the circumstances. The term cosmopolitan appeared in public already during the war and with unmistakable reference to Soviet Jews. [...]« (Weiner 2001, 195)

Many undoubtedly used the »anti-cosmopolitan« purges for their own personal gain, for example to discredit their superiors or colleagues with the allegation of »cosmopolitanism«. However, aside from these kinds of motives, the sense of danger from the outside world, which determined the thinking of politicians and the population in those early years of the Cold War, should not be underestimated.

What were the aims of the Soviet leadership in its fight against »rootless cosmopolitanism«? – In answer to this question, severely diverse motives can be identified:

1. Firstly, the campaign's anti-Semitic line of attack is apparent. This includes both the propaganda, which operated purposefully with anti-Jewish stereotypes like that of the »Jew without a homeland« and the »worldwide Jewish conspiracy«, as well as active repressions, the victims of which mainly derived from the Jewish intelligentsia. As part of the anti-Jewish orientation two differing aims were pursued: the ultimate suppression of all demands of any kind which Soviet Jews may have made for cultural and political autonomy – in whichever shape and form – as well as the intention to provide the population with a familiar scapegoat disguised as cosmopolitanism to blame for the disastrous social, economic and political state of the Soviet Union in the post-war period.
2. The orientation of the campaigns, which were hostile to the intelligentsia, is closely related to the anti-Jewish component. The Soviet leadership, above all those politicians who were in charge of the campaign, Stalin, Zhdanov and Malenkov, saw in the intelligentsia the main enemy and obstacle for the party in obtaining complete control over society. They strove towards the elimination of influential circles of the Soviet intelligentsia, which they found unreliable or easy to manipulate. By making an example of the intelligentsia, the rulers at the same time endeavoured to abolish the social concessions, which they themselves had allowed, or rather, the existence of which they had been unable to prevent during the years of war.
3. Alongside this, the Soviet leadership pursued the aim of ideological and political isolation of the Soviet camp from the West: against the background of the early Cold War the campaigns served as a strategy of isolation. Inner ideological closeness was to be reached through the elimination of all »foreign ideas« and those persons who were »infected« with them. A patriotic disposition had to dominate over a »cosmopolitan spirit« and over »Western decadence«. Accordingly the Jews, who represented a significant proportion of Soviet intelligentsia, aroused suspicion in the regime both as members of the intelligentsia and as potential cosmopolitans.
4. In the course of the purges as part of the anti-cosmopolitan campaigns domestic power struggles took place, above all in the ranks of the state

and party leadership. In the specialist literature the opinion is to be found that Stalin and other members of the Soviet leadership succeeded in entangling their political opponents and rivals in the campaigns to such an extent as to strengthen their own positions.

In the course of the anti-cosmopolitan and anti-Zionist campaigns described here, which extensively fell back on the anti-Semitic construct of pre-revolutionary Russian nationalism, Stalin engraved upon the ideology and politics of the Soviet Union an extremely negative perception of »cosmopolitanism«. This was to undergo no significant changes either in terms of the official portrayal or in the outlook of large sections of Soviet society before the downfall of the Soviet Union. Hence, even in its 23rd edition of 1991, the dictionary of Ozhegov, published by the Russian Academy of Science, still defined the word »cosmopolitan« as follows:

»A reactionary bourgeois ideology, which, disguised by slogans pertaining to a world state and cosmopolitanism [Weltbürgertum], rejects the right of nations to an autonomous existence and state independence and preaches the renouncement of national traditions, a national culture and patriotism.« (Ozhegov 1991, 300)

Even the Marxist-Leninist theory before Stalin had rejected »cosmopolitanism« as a »bourgeois ideology« and instead postulated a »proletarian internationalism«. Nevertheless, it was not until Stalin's change of policy towards fostering a particular Soviet patriotism, which increasingly fed off of an aggressive Russian chauvinism that the ideological basis for the incorporation of anti-cosmopolitanism into the Soviet ideology was laid down.

The Ideology of »Anti-Cosmopolitanism« and Anti-Zionism as an Integral Part of Russian nationalism – A Summary

As has hopefully been made clear, the comparison of the content and function of the cosmopolitanism constructions before 1917 and in the late 1940s under Stalin reveals a whole range of substantial similarities. In summary, I would like, once again, to touch upon the points which in my opinion are the most important:

1. Both the ideology of the Russian Radical Right before 1917 and the anti-cosmopolitanism of the Stalinist era display unmistakable anti-

Jewish and anti-Semitic components. In both historical contexts this served above all as a strategy of integration within the respective camps and as a means of mobilisation against the real or supposed enemy. In both systems the Jews were largely perceived as a minority hostile to the Russian or Soviet »people« and allegedly »scrounging off« them.

The inner contradictoriness of these constructs was to be seen most clearly in the exploitation of anti-Semitism. Thus, in the mentality of the far right before 1917 the Jews were simultaneously considered to be agents of capitalism as well as an incarnation of the revolutionary and intellectual.

2. Both concepts of cosmopolitanism discussed here are ultimately only conceivable in the context of a nationalistic or chauvinistic ideology. Cosmopolitanism served fundamentally as an ideological discursive weapon, which lead to an intensified creation of barriers between the sides and to an aggressive emotional attachment within the friend-enemy-mentality. In this way modern nationalism is opened wider for pre-modern concepts and patterns of thought, which are expressed for example in the anti-Jewish resentments of the Jews as the murderers of Christ and troublemakers. Stalinism shied away no less from this kind of exploitation, which is shown by the so called the »Doctors' Plot« or the »Doctors' affair«, staged at the beginning of 1953.

   Anti-cosmopolitanism can be understood as a specific characteristic of Russian nationalism, which constructed the »rootless« cosmopolitan as an antithesis to the patriotic »true« Russian. Before 1917 this »true« Russian was primarily defined by means of his orthodox beliefs and his identification with autocracy and the Russian idea, while under Stalin he was characterised accordingly as an »orthodox« Soviet patriot loyal to the regime.

3. Furthermore, for both concepts of cosmopolitanism an anti-modern and anti-Western orientation is characteristic and fundamental. In particular the stigmatisation of the West as, amongst other things, »capitalistic«, »rationalistic«, »soulless«, »bourgeois« and »decadent« served as a strategy to set political boundaries, which – before 1917 as well as under Stalin – had the function of discrediting certain states, leading personalities, political ideas or concepts in the eyes of the Russian population. Hence England was demonised before 1917 as the motherland of parliamentarianism, and after 1945, with the Cold War loom-

ing, England and the USA in particular were attacked for their imperialism, capitalism and their decadent culture.

4. Finally, both the far right ideologists before 1917 and those under Stalin saw in cosmopolitanism a »hostile (world) principle« irreconcilably opposed to the Russian idea, a principle which was causing destruction in practically all social areas (politics, economy, culture etc). By this logic, the cosmopolitan was seen as an agent of a *weltanschauung* that differed radically from Russian patriotism. Furthermore, the cosmopolitan was an »agent of foreign powers« within his own country.

The analysis of the concept of anti-cosmopolitanism in the Russian context has made clear that throughout such fundamental historical *caesuras* as the 1917 Revolution there were, and still are, notable ideological continuities. The comparison of significant elements of the ideologies of the Russian Radical Right before 1917 and the Soviet era, in particular of Stalinism, shows that in both systems the »cosmopolitan« was ultimately conceptualised as the sum of all characteristics that appeared highly foreign to the »Russian nature«.

Behind this manner of thinking, an even older important tradition in the Russian history of ideas is discernible: the debates between the so-called Slavophiles and Westernisers about the relationship of Russia and Europe, as well as about Russia's distinctiveness and its world role. The question of whether or not Russia now actually belongs to Europe and what exactly constitutes the Russian nature is to this day at the centre of Russian self-perception and self-image. The development of the concept of anti-cosmopolitanism and then, from the end of the 1940's onwards, of anti-Zionism should be viewed in this context, because to a certain extent it is here that the search for a Russian identity is expressed.

Upon the background of the dramatic political and socio-economical developments and changes since 1861, the Russian nationalism of the Far-Right before 1917 and that of the Stalin-period transformed the negative image of the »rational West«, pertaining to the Slavophile thinkers of the nineteenth century, into a new, politically more aggressive formation of ideas, in which the political anti-Semitism of the late Tsarist era with its delusion of a »Jewish plot to achieve world domination« now represented a main component.

Throughout the Soviet period and until this day the concept of anti-cosmopolitanism or anti-Zionism remains, in slight variations, at the centre of countless identity constructions of Russian parties and groupings, particularly at the right and left ends of the political spectrum. Precisely in view of the effects of globalisation processes, which have become more palpable in Russia since the end of communism, the ideology of anti-cosmopolitanism or anti-Zionism, which operates with simplistic concepts of the enemy and with the allocations of blame, once again in Russian history appears to many politicians and citizens to offer straightforward explanations and solutions.

Works Cited

Anti-Cosmopolitanism. *Time*, 24 November 1961, accessed 11 June 2007 http://www.time.com/time/magazine/article/0,9171,828846,00.html

Baltiiskii, N. (1945). Über den Patriotismus (O patriotizme). *Novoe vremia* 1/11 (1945), 3–11. Quoted in Golczewski and Pickhan 1998, 227–234.

Brokgauz, F.A. and I.A. Efron (eds.). (1895). *Entsiklopedicheskii slovar'*, 16. St. Petersburg: Brokgauz-Efron.

Brooks, Jeffrey (1985). *When Russia Learned to Read: Literacy and Popular Literature, 1861–1917*. Princeton, N.J.: Princeton University Press.

Brooks, Jeffrey (1992). Official Xenophobia and Popular Cosmopolitanism in Early Soviet Russia. *The American Historical Review*, 97/5, 1431–1448.

Dal', Vladimir (1881). *Tolkovyi slovar' zhivogo velikorusskogo jazyka*, 2. St. Petersburg, Moscow: M.O. Vol'f.

Golczewski, Frank, and Gertrud Pickhan (eds.). (1998). *Russischer Nationalismus. Die russische Idee im 19. und 20. Jahrhundert.* Göttingen: Vandenhoeck & Ruprecht.

Goncharov, Ivan (1899). Fregat »Pallada«: ocherki puteshestviia. In *Polnoe sobranie sochinenii*, 5. St. Peterburg: A.F. Marx.

Grüner, Frank (2008). *Patrioten und Kosmopoliten. Juden im Sowjetstaat 1941–1953.* Cologne, Weimar, Vienna: Böhlau Verlag.

Haber, Erich (1992): Cosmopolitanism, antisemitism and Populism: a reappraisal of Russian and Jewish response to pogroms of 1881–1882. In John Klier and Shlomo Lambroza (eds.). *Pogroms: anti-Jewish violence in modern Russian History*, 98–134. Cambridge (et al.): Cambridge University Press.

Hahn, Werner G. (1982): *Postwar Soviet Politics: The Fall of Zhdanov and the Defeat of Moderation, 1946–53.* Ithaca/N.Y.: Cornell University Press.

Kostyrchenko, Gennadii V. (2001). *Tainaia politika Stalina: Vlast' i antisemitizm.* Moscow: Mezhdunarodnye otnosheniia.

Löwe, Heinz-Dietrich (1978). *Antisemitismus und reaktionare Utopie. Russischer Konservatismus im Kampf gegen den Wandel von Staat und Gesellschaft.* Hamburg: Hoffmann und Campe.

Löwe, Heinz-Dietrich (1993). *The Tsars and the Jews. Reform, Reaction and Anti-Semitism in Imperial Russia, 1772–1917*. Chur: Harwood Academic Publishers.

Ozhegov, S.I. (1991). *Slovar' russkogo jazyka*. 23. Revised edition. Published by the Institute for Russian Language of the Academy of Science of the USSR. Moscow: Russkii jazyk.

Rogger, Hans (1986). *Jewish Policies and Right-Wing Politics in Imperial Russia*. Berkeley (et al.): University of California Press.

Weiner, Amir (2001). *Making Sense of War: the Second World War and the Fate of the Bolshevik Revolution*. Princeton: Princeton University Press.

Between Nationalism and Internationalism: Displaced Persons at the UNRRA University of Munich

Anna Holian

In the first years after World War II, Munich was home to a unique institution known as the UNRRA University.[1] Situated in the heart of the city at the famed *Deutsches Museum* of science and technology, the university was created by displaced persons (DPs), the multinational population of concentration camp survivors, former forced laborers, and refugees from Eastern Europe who found themselves in Germany at war's end.[2] Named after its main sponsor, the United Nations Relief and Rehabilitation Administration, it began as a series of lectures and language courses in the summer of 1945. One of many educational projects started by displaced persons in postwar Europe, it was distinguished by its multinational population of students and professors and by its internationalist ethos. At its height, it had more than 2,000 students representing 28 different »nationalities«, with the majority drawn from the ranks of Ukrainian, Polish, Lithuanian, Russian, Latvian and Jewish DPs. The university's proponents defined it as a new kind of educational institution, dedicated to reviving humanism and internationalism. In the words of student leader Eduard Alperovitch, it would serve as »a training ground for cosmopolitanism« (Alperowitsch 1948). Despite hopes of making it a permanent institution, the university only lasted a short time. UNRRA withdrew its support in the spring of 1947, and attempts to solicit aid from other sources failed. The university finally folded in September 1948.

An earlier version of this essay appeared as »Displacement and the Post-war Reconstruction of Education: Displaced Persons at the UNRRA University of Munich, 1945–1948«, in *Contemporary European History* 17:2 (May 2008), 167–195, copyright Cambridge University Press.

1 On the history of the university, see also Zittel 1979.

2 The term »displaced person« was used by the Allies to refer to »civilians outside the national boundaries of their country by reason of the war«. On DP policies and practices, see Proudfoot 1956.

The relationship between displacement and identity has received a great deal of attention in recent years (Bammer 1994; Lavie and Swedenburg 1996; Gupta and Ferguson 1997; Clifford 1992; Malkki 1995; Ong 1999). While early discussions around this issue focused on contemporary developments, and were often intimately connected to arguments about globalisation as a process of accelerating mobility, increasingly scholars are also looking backwards, examining the role that migration and displacement have played in the making of societies and communities past. For historians of the twentieth century, the migrant and the refugee have emerged as central figures of political history, to borrow a phrase from philosopher Giorgio Agamben (Agamben 2000, section 21). Growing interest in the history of migrants and refugees has been coupled with a new analytic attention to the ways in which displacement challenges conventional narratives about cultural identity. Indeed, as Liisa Malkki notes, the growth of interest in displacement and its effects may have less to do with empirical shifts than with new ways of thinking about the relationship between people, place and identity. Moving away from looking at culture as a »rooted« phenomenon with its own home territory, scholars are increasingly attuned to »the complexity of ways in which people construct, remember, and lay claim to particular places as ›homelands‹ or ›nations‹ « (Malkki 1992, 25). This perspective has informed much recent work, which examines how experiences of migration and exile strengthen, transform and undermine existing cultural and especially national attachments.

At first glance, the history of Europe's displaced persons would appear to be a clear case of migration strengthening existing national identifications. According to many contemporary observers, DPs were fiercely nationalistic. Filmmaker Fred Zinnemann, for example, who visited DP camps in Germany in 1947, was struck by the total lack of solidarity among what he called »the remnants of various decimated nationalities.« In his estimation, »all were victims of extreme nationalism« (Zinnemann 1992, 59–61). The philosopher Hannah Arendt put things even more strongly. »Not a single group of refugees or Displaced Persons«, she wrote, »has failed to develop a fierce, violent group consciousness and to clamor for rights as – and only as – Poles or Jews or Germans, etc« (Arendt 1973, 292). Echoing these comments, historian Wolfgang Jacobmeyer has suggested that nationality was »the only great concept in the consciousness of the DPs« (Jacobmeyer 1985, 51).

Although nationalism was indeed a potent force among displaced persons, the focus on nationalism has also distracted from other important developments, including nascent forms of internationalism. Here the brief but turbulent history of the UNRRA University is illuminating. It suggests how experiences of displacement encouraged the development of new transnational alliances and imaginaries. An imagined *international* community of displaced persons emerged, one aimed at transcending what contemporaries defined as the three main categories of difference: nationality, religion and race. The development of this international community was encouraged by the postwar conditions of displacement, which created a DP forced community that shared a number of interests and experiences. It was also a manifestation of the broader postwar resurgence of internationalist thinking. In establishing the university, displaced persons were thus not only responding to the peculiarities of their predicament, they were also participating in a broader movement to internationalise postwar education. Indeed, the university represents an important grassroots example of international education, as it was one of the only international university projects conceived during this period that saw the light of day.

At the same time, the history of the UNRRA University suggests that internationalism is not always the antithesis of nationalism. Rather, these two modes of thinking about belonging can be mutually reinforcing. Although some of the university's participants were idealistic promoters of a cosmopolitan point of view, others were deeply involved in national politics. Some were affiliated with radical nationalist movements. This is not as paradoxical as it may at first appear. The liberal model of internationalism that predominated at the university identified nations as the building blocks of the world community. It viewed peaceful coexistence between nations as the foundation of peace more generally. It thus tended to reaffirm rather than challenge the centrality of national categories. This understanding of internationalism appealed to displaced persons, who often saw themselves as nationals in exile. Indeed, by mimicking the structures of the emerging postwar international community, most notably the United Nations, the university provided DPs with a framework in which they could affirm their national identifications – and, just as importantly, have these identifications recognised by others – despite the fact that they now stood outside the official »national order of things.«[3] Far from representing a

3 I borrow this phrase from Malkki (1995).

clear antithesis to nationalism, then, internationalism was to some extent its logical extension.

The Rise and Fall of the UNRRA University

The UNRRA University emerged out of the DP camp established by UNRRA at the *Deutsches Museum.* By the summer of 1945, the *Museum* had become known as a gathering place for academically-minded DPs. [4] In August 1945, these DPs created an organisation called International Academic Self-Help (*Internationale Akademische Selbsthilfe*) and began holding courses. Designed for students whose university studies had been interrupted by the war, as well as for those who had not been able to finish their secondary education, the courses covered a wide array of topics, including experimental physics, analytic geometry, ethics, commercial law and modern German literature. English and Spanish language courses were also offered. According to a report from September 1945, the courses drew 471 students.[5] Most likely, the initial intention was not to create a university.[6] Indeed, the courses were to some extent intended to prepare students for *German* universities, which, in the American and British zones, were required to set aside 10 percent of all places for DPs. At the same time, it was clear that the 10 percent quota would not accommodate all DPs who wanted to study.[7] This consideration no doubt helped push the project forward. By October 1945, it had been defined as a university.[8] The official opening took place in February 1946.

According to the university's statutes, there were nine faculties: Philosophy, Law, Economics, Natural Sciences, Medicine, Veterinary Medicine,

---

4 Memorandum re: »Education – Lectures for Students«, 11 September 1945, United Nations Archives (hereafter UNA), United Nations Relief and Rehabilitation Administration Records (hereafter UNRRA), 3.0.11.3.2, Box 33, T 108.

5 »The List of the Registered Students«, n.d.; »Academical Section Report«, 11 September 1945, UNA, UNRRA, S-0436-0031-03.

6 »Die neue UNRRA-Universität in München«, n.d., Bayerisches Hauptstaatsarchiv (hereafter BayHStA), Bestand UNRRA-Universität (hereafter UU) 2.

7 »The story of the UNRRA University«, n.d., UNA, UNRRA, 3.0.11.0.1.4, Box 2, Displaced Persons University – Munich.

8 W.S. Rogers to Miss Richman, 31 October 1945, UNA, UNRRA, 3.0.11.3.2, Box 33, T 108.

Civil Engineering, Mechanical Engineering, Agriculture and Forestry.[9] However, some of these existed only on paper. The Faculty of Philosophy, viewed as the capstone of the university, never opened because it lacked qualified personnel. The same was true of a planned Faculty of Theology. Programmes that depended on specialised facilities such as laboratories had an especially difficult time functioning. Students and faculty often had to create these facilities from scratch. The lingua franca at the university was German, but not everyone knew the language well.

The student body at the university reflected the disruptive effects of the war. Most students had begun their studies before the war. Many had spent time in forced labor, concentration, and prisoner-of-war camps. The result was an unusual age distribution, with students between twenty-one and twenty-five years of age making up the largest age cohort (45 percent), followed by students between twenty-six and thirty (19 percent).[10] Women made up about 30 percent of the student body, compared to about 13 percent at German universities.[11] According to the records for the summer semester of 1946, the largest groups were Ukrainians (649 students), Poles (348), Lithuanians (297), Russians (233), Latvians (210), Jews (134), Byelorussians (122) and Estonians (115). Only *bona fide* displaced persons could study at the university, meaning Allied nationals with no history of involvement in war crimes.

While the student body was limited to DPs, the faculty also included non-DPs, brought in to supplement the limited number of qualified DP professors.[12] Most faculty members had been educated in continental Europe. Some had worked in Germany, German-occupied territories, or German-allied countries during the war. For example, the Russian *émigré* zoologist Mikhail Mikhailovich Novikov, Dean of Natural Sciences, had worked at the University of Bratislava during the war (Novikov 1952, 362–3). Other professors, like the Slovene jurist Otmar Pirkmajer, who was

---

9 »Statut der UNRRA-Universität-München«, (March 1946), BayHStA, UU 4.

10 »UNRRA University«, 30 November 1946, UNA, UNRRA, 3.0.11.3.0, Box 65, Welfare – Education – Zone Director's File on Deutsches Museum.

11 Statistics on women at the UNRRA University come from »UNRRA University Munich«, n.d., BayHStA, UU 28; those on women at German universities come from CEWS-Statistikportal, »Entwicklung des Studentinnenanteils in Deutschland seit 1908«, http://www.cews.org/statistik/hochschulen.php?aid=20&cid=16 (accessed 8 September 2006).

12 Memorandum from W.S. Rogers to the Rector, UNRRA University, 1 February 1946, UNA, UNRRA, S-0425-0062-01.

eventually selected as rector of the university, had participated in the anti-fascist resistance and been interned in concentration camps. Numerically, the faculty was dominated by Russians (31 percent) and Ukrainians (23 percent). Only three faculty members were Jewish. Most strikingly, Russians dominated at the rank of full professor (occupying ten of the 27 chairs) and among the deans. This mixed picture is no doubt in part the product of Nazi efforts to destroy national elites in the occupied countries. Hence those who had collaborated or at least accommodated themselves to Nazi occupation were more likely to have survived into the postwar.

Despite moving towards ever greater legitimacy, the university struggled to establish itself. The most serious problem was not the lack of funds or equipment but rather the difficulty of squaring the university with the Allied DP program. According to Boris Balinsky, a former professor at the university, »UNRRA obviously did not know what to do with the University in the long run.« (Balinsky 1982).[13] Although local UNRRA and Army officials enthusiastically supported it, broader policy objectives worked against it. The Allies wanted to see displaced persons repatriated as quickly as possible. UNRRA's mandate was to facilitate this process. Little thought was given to the problem of so-called »non-repatriable« DPs. Indeed, in an effort to compel them to return, their existence was wilfully ignored. As UNRRA personnel acknowledged, the university's relationship to the goal of repatriation was »very slight«.[14] Moreover, the university seemed to pose a deterrent to repatriation. Although there was »no overpowering evidence« of an organised anti-repatriation campaign, many students and professors were clearly unwilling to returning home.[15] It was also evident that establishing the university on a more permanent basis would have »unsatisfactory implications« for the repatriation program.[16]

Acting on these concerns, in December 1946 UNRRA announced that it was withdrawing its support.[17] The following month, it ordered the

13 I am grateful to Mark Wyman for providing me with a copy of this text.

14 »Conference about UNRRA University«, (June 1946), UNA, UNRRA, S-0412, Box 10, File 1.

15 Memorandum to R.W. Collins re: »Deutsches Museum, UNRRA University«, 4 December 1946, UNA, UNRRA, S-0425-0065-08.

16 Yngve Frykholm, »The UNRRA University at Munich«, June 1946, UNA, UNRRA, 3.0.11.0.1.4, Box 2.

17 Memorandum from J.H. Whiting to S. Zisman, 16 December 1946, UNA, UNRRA, 3.0.11.3.1, District 5 – Education.

university to vacate the *Deutsches Museum*.[18] A student protest succeeded in convincing the U.S. Military Government to allow the university to operate until the end of the winter semester. In May 1947, the university officially closed. Throughout the rest of 1947 and into 1948, its most dedicated students and faculty promoters searched for new sponsors, soliciting aid from governments, intergovernmental agencies, religious organisations, and other universities. At the same time, they lobbied for students and faculty to be accepted into German universities and sought opportunities to emigrate. For a while, it seemed that the university might be revived under the sponsorship of the German organisation *Pro Una Sancta Ecclesia*, whose plans were supported by the *Bavarian Ministry for Education and Culture*. However, these plans fell through. In September 1948, students and faculty gave up on reviving the UNRRA University. Many students continued studying at German universities. Most eventually left Germany for the United States, Canada, Israel and other countries.

War and the New International Humanist University

From an early point, the university's organisers focused not only on putting their institution on firm academic, financial, and legal footing, but also on defining the university project to themselves and the outside world. The UNRRA University, they argued, was something »more« than a DP university; conversely, a DP university was something »more« than an average university. They presented the university as a new kind of international institution dedicated to the revival of humanism, interpreted as a defense of modern liberal and democratic ideals. They juxtaposed this model not only against National Socialism, but also Soviet communism. Their conception of the university was thus informed by both antifascism and anticommunism.

In talking about their commitment to humanism, the university's proponents stressed their desire to recuperate an older university tradition. The UNRRA University, they claimed, represented a return to the humanist principles that had motivated the creation of universities before the modern era. They narrated the history of the university idea in terms of a

18 UNRRA University to Van Steenberg, 14 January 1947, BayHStA, UU 45.

progressive abandonment of liberal humanism, with its commitment to making the university the sum of human knowledge. According to this interpretation, »the Universitarian idea [...] has passed the stages of a transformation from liberal University to national University, from humanistic to political University.«[19] As a consequence, »the universal character of the idea of University has lost much of its [...] importance« and »the prevailing tendency was the safeguarding of national and political aims and interests.«[20] At the same time, the return to an older humanist tradition was also an embrace of modern human rights. According to the rector Otmar Pirkmajer, the UNRRA University »will show the students their way to critical observations and nurse the sense for the reality of things without undermining the idealism. The DP student should become bearer of Idea, Moral, Truth, Justice, Freedom and Humanity.«[21]

The goal of promoting humanism was closely associated with internationalism. Modern internationalism, the university suggested, was commensurate with medieval humanism, because »science and art have in all ages been international.«[22] Hence the creation of an international university was the realisation of an ancient ideal. Indeed, it was the best means of »further[ing] the evolution in the reverse direction« and recuperating the universal character of the university lost with the development of nationalism.[23] The university and the nation-state, student leader Eduard Alperovitch argued, were based on fundamentally different principles. The modern state served utilitarian purposes, while the university was concerned with the world of the »spirit« (Alperowitsch 1948). Thus only an international institution could truly realise the original idea of the university.

Internationalism, it needs to be recalled, has multiple meanings, reflecting the diversity of ideas that have been placed under its *aegis*. Of central importance here is the distinction between liberal and cosmopolitan internationalism. According to *liberal internationalism*, the world is composed of discrete nations, and the maintenance of good relations among nations is the basis for improving relations among individuals. This form of inter-

19 »Sources of Legal Status of UNRRA University«, n.d., BayHStA, UU 1.

20 Ibid.

21 »The Official Speech of the Rector at the Unaugural [sic] Ceremony of the UNRRA-University«, n.d., UNA, UNRRA, 3.0.11.0.1.4, Box 2, Displaced Persons University – Munich.

22 Provisorisches Studentenkomitee to the student body, 11 July 1946, BayHStA, UU 3.

23 »Sources of Legal Status«.

nationalism thus takes the existence of nations for granted. Indeed, as Jonathan Rée argues, it produces the nation form, making it possible to assign each person and each territory a definite nationality (Rée 1992, 9; see also Malkki 1994, 56). According to *cosmopolitan internationalism*, on the other hand, the world is a community of individual »world citizens«. Here differences of nationality do not come into play and may in fact be transcended. Here internationalism means »a willingness to overlook national interest in favor of the welfare of humanity as a whole.« (Rée 1992, 10). These two forms of internationalism are not easily distinguished and in practice are often intertwined. This was certainly the case at the UNRRA University, where the vision of a supranational community was often taken to mean cooperation between individuals of different nationalities.

The university's commitment to internationalism was often presented as a product of the war. In particular, it was presented a response to National Socialism. Writing to the U.S. military authorities in December 1945, the organisers of the *International Students' Association* (ISA) argued that an international organisation was the best means of way of reconstructing scholarship in the aftermath of National Socialism. The »foreign students«, they argued,

> »should like to contest the tendency of the former-regime which introduced the element of exclusiveness not only into national life but also in the scientific domain. The foreign young generation understood quite clearly that [in] trying to attain scientific purposes the collaboration is the first condition for a successful enterprise. The foreign students pursuing scientific aims are therefore ready to collaborate in the name of humanitarian and scientific ideals.«[24]

An international organisation, they maintained,

> »gives the possibility to act in a way free of selfishness and full of esteem for human personality and with the consciousness that scientific and cultural good are universal, to which no particular person or nation could lay claims. Just the misunderstanding of this truth was one of the causes of the outbreak of the world war«.[25]

The commitment to internationalism thus represented an indictment of national chauvinism in general and National Socialism in particular.

At the same time, the university's participants also suggested that the experience of living under National Socialism had taught them the value of international cooperation. Employing the language of antifascism, they

24 »Group of iniciators« to William Rogers, 14 December 1945, BayHStA, UU 5755.
25 Ibid.

argued that the Nazis had not only destroyed nations but also brought into being new forms of international solidarity. According to the UNRRA University Students' Union,

»young people who got to know one another in the concentration camps and work camps, almost all placed by fate in the same situation, now work together towards the realization of new ideals, towards the creation of new values. They offer the bitter experience of their youth to the world, so that there will never again be people who are persecuted because of their religious, national or racial belonging«.[26]

Here the Nazi concentration and forced labor camps were identified as sites of internationalist formation. The experience of persecution was represented as a shared one – a kind of enforced identification, which taught the students to respect one another.

Although the turn to internationalism was often rhetorically linked to antifascism, anticommunism played an equally if not more important role in uniting the university's participants – or, at least, its non-Jewish ones. During the university's existence, anticommunism by necessity remained muted, since the United States was at this time still allied with the Soviet Union. Nonetheless, evidence of anticommunist sentiment can be found between the lines of many documents, especially in references to »democracy«. For example, a formal statement about the university noted that its participants included not only former concentration camps prisoners, foreign workers and prisoners of war, but also »persons who have abandoned their countries having fled from their political enemies because of their democratic convictions«. Here refugees from Eastern Europe were presented as principled opponents of communism and other »undemocratic« movements.[27] Similarly, in a 1946 interview with psychologist David Boder, student leader Valerius Michelson suggested that his interest in building an international university grew out of his wartime observations of disunity among »the people from the East«. »And it appeared to me«, he told Boder,

»that in this university we, the youth, who after sufficient preparation will become the leaders in their own countries, [...] if we should be friends among ourselves we would be able to create a rapprochement between our countries to an extent nec-

26 UNRRA University Students' Union to the Bavarian Ministry for Education and Cultural Affairs, 17 December 1946, BayHStA, MK 68753.

27 »UNRRA University Munich«,

essay in order that there would be neither wars nor these horrible totalitarian regimes which humiliate man and [oppress] his abilities to think and to create for the good of other men«. (Michelson 1946)

Although Michelson's argument was not merely anticommunist, the references to totalitarianism and to future leadership suggest that one of the unifying forces at the university was the desire to see a post-»totalitarian« Eastern Europe.

After the university's official closing, anticommunism emerged more clearly. Indeed, letters to potential sponsors sometimes presented the university's troubles as the product of communist machinations.[28] Anticommunism also features prominently in retrospective accounts. Thus Boris Pawlow, an old Russian *émigré* who worked as a research assistant at the university, writes in a 1985 article that internationality did not pose a problem because »all felt united by the work and by the communist danger in the immediate vicinity« (Pawlow 1985, 92). Similarly, Borys Daniluk, a former student of Byelorussian nationality, notes that the harmony among the students was due largely to shared attitudes towards the Soviet Union.[29] Missing from this harmonious image are Jewish DPs, who did not view communism as a major threat and may well have found the anticommunism of other DPs worrisome due to its common and pernicious associations with antisemitism. Indeed, in the aftermath of the Holocaust, it was hard not to think about anticommunism without summoning up recollections of the Nazi campaign against »Judeo-Bolshevism«.

While the emphasis on cooperation between nationalities conforms to a liberal conception of internationalism, the university's participants also occasionally gestured in the direction of cosmopolitanism. »The development of relations«, an essay on the university argued,

»will never move in the direction of real good will and cooperation, will never lead to a continental citizenship or even to a world citizenship, unless the idea of the collaboration and coexistence of nations paves the way for a supranational and supraideological understanding«.[30]

Here, then, internationalism was presented as a stepping stone towards cosmopolitanism. A more forceful statement of the cosmopolitan vision

28 Liquidation Board to William C. Bullit, August 1948; Liquidation Board to U. Carusi, 10 September 1948, BayHStA, UU 48.

29 Borys Daniluk, letter to author, 8 November 2004.

30 Untitled essay on the International University, n.d., BayHStA, UU 3.

was presented by the university's rector Otmar Pirkmajer. Speaking at the university's opening ceremony in February 1946, Pirkmajer identified the university as a training ground for a new postwar cosmopolitan *élite*. The university, he argued, would provide the DP student with

»a wide horizon and the magnanimous power of judgment of a cosmopolitan. [...] The new intellectual man must have interest in and understanding for the burning questions of the universal cultural life, for the important currents of thought and for the outlines and inner relations of the whole culture at large. The UNRRA University which possesses as an international institution supernational [*sic*] character, will be in a position to affect in this particular direction, as, she, without any consideration for political or national characteristics, will try to impart to the students the universally recognized teachings and scientific researches and try to draw their attention more to the cardinal points than to the trivial details«.[31]

Representations of the university as a cosmopolitan institution drew on the idea that displaced persons had lost their national attachments by virtue of having been displaced. DP-ness was interpreted as a form of homelessness, which compelled DPs to develop new supranational identifications. In short, displacement led to cosmopolitanism. The DP student, Pirkmajer argued,

»will have to bear in mind that the wide world with all its problems has become his home and that he has to adapt all his interest, all his faculties of thinking and all his knowledge to this one fact. The UNRRA University can, therefore, in no way be an institution with national or locally limited aims«.[32]

Unlike the philosopher Theodor Adorno, who argued that today »it is part of morality not to be at home in one's home«. Pirkmajer did not view homelessness as an intellectual responsibility (Adorno 1978, 39). Nonetheless, he believed the university could make a virtue of necessity.

Despite these gestures in the direction of cosmopolitanism, for the most part the university's participants hewed to a liberal model of internationalism. Indeed, they engaged in elaborate processes of national classification and representation. The university's formal statements consistently emphasised the multinational quality of the student body and provided statistics for each national group. Similarly, the university's student groups were organised along the lines of the United Nations, with each nationality receiving a single »mandate«. Thus, although the university's participants

31 »The Official Speech of the Rector.« See footnote 22.
32 Ibid.

were keen to eliminate what they saw as national chauvinism, they were by no means opposed to »healthy« national attachments. Many of the university's participants were in fact staunch nationalists. Law professor George Studynsky, for example, was affiliated with the *Organisation of Ukrainian Nationalists*, a radical nationalist movement which sought to create a Ukrainian state along »pure« ethnonational lines. Despite the fact that he himself had enjoyed an international education, attending institutions in Vienna, Graz, and Paris, he was wary of internationalism. Speaking at a conference of Ukrainian emigrants in November 1949, Studynsky argued that it was easy to collaborate on »DP matters« but not on »issues of cardinal importance«. »All those gentlemen, who happily sign when it has to do with the protection of some Ukrainian camp«, he argued, »these same gentlemen spread deception on the Ukrainian issue among the IRO and other [national] groups.« Thus although Ukrainians could not afford to alienate other nationalities, they had to be »very careful« (Protocol 1949). Internationalism could not be allowed to interfere with national interests.

Indeed, for many of the university's participants, the appeal of internationalism lay precisely in the fact that it could be harmonised with nationalism. This was of course a delicate balancing act, but it was better than the alternative, namely national isolation. Identifying nationalities as the building blocks of the world community, the liberal model of internationalism reaffirmed the centrality of national belonging. Simultaneously, it offered each nationality a seat at the table. It thus provided displaced persons with an alternative source of national recognition – a new international community. It also allowed them to assert national affiliations that had no official standing because they did not correspond to recognised states. This appealed equally to DPs who had effectively lost their states (e.g., Lithuanians, Latvians, and Estonians); to those who viewed their states as illegitimate (e.g., Poles); and to those who had not (yet) been able to acquire one (e.g., Jews and Ukrainians).

The Practice of International Cooperation: Jews and Non-Jews

As we have seen, the university's claims to internationality were premised in part on the diversity of its participants. Indeed, the university frequently noted its desire to transcend what contemporaries defined as the three main categories of difference, namely, nationality, religion, and race. How did this work in practice? To what extent did the university succeed in creating the atmosphere of tolerance and friendship it advertised? What tensions did the concept of internationalism obscure? One way of addressing this issue is by looking at relations between Jews and non-Jews. Jewish experiences of the war differed fundamentally from those of non-Jews. Moreover, the mass murder of European Jewry had taken place under the eyes of, and often with the assistance of, non-Jewish Eastern Europeans. For many Jewish survivors, it was thus inconceivable to return to their home communities – or to live among non-Jews in the DP camps. At the university, however, Jewish and non-Jewish DPs worked in intimate proximity. The university thus provides a window onto relations between Jews and non-Jews in the aftermath of the Holocaust.

The university's proponents generally avoided making qualitative distinctions between different groups. In keeping with the internationalist idea, all participants were presented as equals in a horizontal community of suffering. Jewish wartime experiences were thus framed as variations on a general theme. Occasionally, the university suggested that Jewish suffering had been extraordinary. In a letter to United Nations Secretary General Trygve Lie, for example, the university's representatives emphasised the fate of Jews in the concentration camps.[33] Jews were also promised priority in admittance to the university because, as the administration acknowledged, they had »suffered most« during the war years.[34] In general, however, national narratives were subordinated to a larger international narrative that smoothed out the differences between wartime histories.

As for Jewish DPs themselves, their attitude towards the university can best be described as ambivalent.[35] On the one hand, Jewish students attended the university in large numbers. In June 1946, 117 of the 196 students registered with the *Jewish Students Union* attended the UNRRA University.[36] Jews also made up one of the largest groups of students at the

---

33 UNRRA University Senate and Administration to Trygve Lie, n.d., BayHStA, UU 54.

34 »Declaration«, 23 January 1947; P. Popoff to Vachtel, 23 January 1947, BayHStA, UU 45.

35 On Jewish DPs students, see (Brodzki and Varon 2005).

36 »Aufstellung aller registrierten Studenten bis 2. Juni 1946«; »Aufstellung der jüdischen Studenten der UNRRA-Universität v. 24.6.46«, YIVO Institute for Jewish Research (hereafter YIVO) 294.2, folder 1227.

university. In September 1946, they were the sixth largest group.[37] Some Jewish students participated enthusiastically in the university. One of the leading figures among the students was Eduard Alperovitch, a Holocaust survivor from Latvia. For him the university represented a repudiation of the racist thinking promoted by the Nazis, and he worked tirelessly to bring the university into being. Other Jewish students also saw the university as a repudiation of racism and nationalism. In a 1946 interview with David Boder, Holocaust survivor Roma Tcharnobroda suggested that the university had succeeded in creating an atmosphere of supranational friendship. »I am very satisfied with the university«, she told Boder. »The relations between professors and students is so great, that indeed one could not find it at any other university.« Asked specifically how she got along with other students, she continued: »Very well. It is interesting. One was able to see that it is possible to live together. And when man lives with man then nationality plays no part. What matters is the person not the nationality« (Tscharnobroda 1946).

On the other hand, many Jewish students did not share this view. They participated in the university because it offered them the chance to study, not because they supported its broader ideological goals or found the atmosphere congenial. Indeed, many deeply resented having to study at the university. Like other Jewish DPs, they viewed non-Jewish Eastern Europeans primarily as participants in the murder of European Jewry and thus did not want to have anything to do with them. As the Jewish Students Union stated in a letter to Albert Einstein,

> »we are forced to study with those who just yesterday were our murderers (together with Germans at the Munich University, the Technical University and so on), or with Latvians, Lithuanians, Poles, Ukrainians, Slovaks etc., among whom the majority were the able helpers of the Germans during the ghetto liquidations and colonizations.«[38]

Jewish students who promoted the university thus had to contend with harsh criticism from other Jews. As Eduard Alperovitch notes, he was criticised by members of the *Jewish Students Union* for associating »with Ukrainians and such people, who are to be shunned and avoided«.[39]

37 Memorandum from Finn Dahle to Mrs. Gaszynska, 16 September 1946, UNA, UNRRA, S-0436-0031-02.

38 Jewish Students Union to Albert Einstein, n.d., YIVO 294.2, folder 1197.

39 Edward Anders (formerly Alperovitch), interview with author, 25 September 2002.

In fact, Jewish students and professors had good reason to be suspicious of their non-Jewish colleagues. Many of the university's participants had less than impeccable wartime records. Some, like the Russian *émigrés* Mikhail Mikhailovich Novikov and Boris Balinsky, can be seen as administrative collaborators, while others may well have been directly involved in the persecution and murder of European Jewry. This possibility emerged clearly in February 1946, when the president of the university's student council, a Ukrainian named Suchenko, was unmasked as a former SS member. The revelation, made only days before the university's official opening, cast doubt on the project as a whole. Especially disturbing was the fact that Suchenko had »worked hard for the establishment of the University«.[40] Indeed, he had participated in creating the first student organisation and had spoken of the need to »cultivate comradeship between the peoples«.[41] His unmasking thus called into question the university's claims to promote international cooperation. If a member of the SS could wave the banner of internationalism, what kind of internationalism did the university represent?

The Suchenko case may have been on the minds of the university's Jewish participants when they met to discuss the future of the university in late 1946. Speaking on behalf of Jews, the *Central Committee of Liberated Jews* voiced cautious support for the university. In a resolution read to the gathered planners, it affirmed that Jews wished to participate, as one nation among many, »in the realization of the fine idea of bringing into being an International University« (Protocol 1946). The ideals of the university, it averred, conformed to those of the Jewish people. »As representatives of that people which suffered most from fascism«, the Committee stated, »we feel ourselves first and foremost responsible for freedom, progress, equality before the law and democracy.« (Ibid.) At the same time, the Central Committee questioned the university's commitment to democracy. It would only participate »if assurance is given that this University will in no way be a haven for conquered but not yet eradicated fascist elements.« (Ibid.)

The university's director responded positively to this call for political housecleaning. However, nothing came of this meeting. After UNRRA's withdrawal, most Jewish students drifted away. Increasingly, the university was presented as an institution promoting western Christian values, a vi-

40 O.A. Nelson to Mr. Whiting, 20 February 1946, UNA, UNRRA, 3.0.11.3.0, Camps, Box 1.

41 »Protocol of the foundation-assembly of the Foreign Students' Association«, n.d., BayHStA, UU 5755.

sion more in keeping with conservative anticommunism than progressive antifascism. Although Eduard Alperovitch remained committed to reviving the university, this conceptualisation of the project clearly had little appeal to most Jewish DPs.

The Sources of Internationalism

In its emphasis on internationalism, and its linkage of internationalism with universal human values, the university mirrored broader contemporary trends. The 1940s saw a resurgence of interest in Europeanist and internationalist projects. The formation of the United Nations at war's end suggested that a new era of international cooperation was about to begin. In the field of education, the key development was the formation of the *United Nations Educational, Scientific, and Cultural Organisation* (UNESCO), which was widely expected to spearhead the formation of an international university (Zweig 1967, 53–62). Students and faculty in Munich were buoyed by these developments. They not only styled themselves as carriers of the »UNO idea«, they also petitioned UNESCO for support, suggesting that their institution could serve as the kernel of a new UNESCO university.[42] The head of UNESCO's Natural Sciences Division, British scientist and sinologist Joseph Needham, even visited the university, though support was not forthcoming (Balinsky 1982).

At the same time, the university's embrace of international education also had more local origins. First, as I have already suggested, students and faculty identified the international idea as a product of their common wartime experiences and postwar aspirations. They presented themselves as a community bound together by experiences of oppression, persecution and opposition to both National Socialism and Soviet communism. These claims can hardly be taken at face value. Nonetheless, both antifascism and anticommunism arguably created a sense of identification among students and faculty, even as they divided them into different camps.[43] Second, the

42 Provisorisches Studentenkomitee to the student body, 11 July 1946; »Memorandum. Concerning: History, Scope and Future of the UNRRA University in Munich, Germany«, 16 December 1946, BayHStA, UU 3.

43 The negative quality of these identifications led some observers to doubt whether it was worthwhile supporting the university. Explaining why his institution did not want to

university's participants were united in their status as members of the forced community of displaced persons. Their status as displaced persons placed them within a common framework of policies and practices in postwar Germany. It created a set of shared interests and problems. One specific problem, of central importance here, concerned access to the universities. Displaced persons stood outside the bounds of the German university system. They not only faced hostility from German colleagues, who viewed them as unwanted »foreigners«, but also definite limits on participation. For DP students, the main problem was the 10 percent quota mentioned earlier. For DP professors, it was access pure and simple. To some extent, then, the university's internationalism can be read as an effort to reframe the forced community of displaced persons as a voluntary community based upon principled commitment to international cooperation.

The framework for managing the DP population also reinforced the centrality of internationalism, especially its liberal variant. On the one hand, the Allied occupation authorities and UNRRA continuously defined displaced persons as members of distinct national groups. This practice was initially intended to facilitate repatriation, but it persisted long after the repatriation programme began to break down, suggesting that the impulse to classify DPs according to nationality went far beyond the merely practical. Indeed, the use of national categories was central to many aspects of UNRRA's programme, from counting the residents of the DP camps to displaying DP handicrafts. These practices presented displaced persons as a »family of nations« – a collective of distinctive yet fundamentally similar groups. On the other hand, UNRRA itself was an international institution. Its existence suggested that the emerging postwar international community was committed to taking care of displaced persons and helping them rebuild their lives. Many of its fieldworkers were idealistic Europeans and Americans, who sincerely believed that international cooperation was the pathway to peace in postwar Europe. In this context, it is not surprising that DP students and professors would have decided that internationalism was the best means of conceptualising their project.[44] Both practically and

fund the university, a represenative of *World Student Relief* noted that »[c]ertain political resentments knit all the DPs of different nationalities together.« Although he did not elaborate, one can surmise that his comments referred to resentment of Germans and/or Soviets. Lars Nyberg to UNRRA University Director, 25 October 1946, BayHStA, UU 3.

44 On refugees and internationalism in a different context, see (Malkki 1994, 46–9).

ideologically, the structures established to manage the DP population reinforced the centrality of internationalism.

Conclusion

The UNRRA University was a product of the early postwar moment, when many displaced persons sat stranded between past and future, unwilling to return home yet unable to resettle elsewhere. Initially conceived as temporary, it developed into an ambitious project to reconceive higher education for the postwar world. The university was defined as an institution committed to the revival of humanism, interpreted as the defence of modern democratic and liberal ideals. Internationalism was identified as the best means of realising the humanist ideal.

The history of the UNRRA University suggests that the prevailing image of displaced persons as ardent nationalists needs to be revised. The university was an important site for the articulation of an internationalist vision of community among DPs. This vision was informed by the contemporary enthusiasm for internationalism and by the specific circumstances of displacement, which encouraged displaced persons to see each other as members of a single community. At the same time, the university's internationalism was itself not a clear repudiation of nationalism. The liberal variant of internationalism that predominated at the university represented displaced persons as a »family of nations«. As my examination of relations between Jewish and non-Jewish DPs suggests, however, internationalism could not paper over the deep divides among DPs. While some Jewish DPs viewed the university as a welcome space of inter- and supranational dialogue, and internationalism itself as the path to a post-fascist future, others resented having to work with non-Jewish DPs, whom they viewed as participants in the murder of European Jewry. The effort to create a new international community thus had to contend with the deeply divided memories of violence and victimisation during the Second World War.

Works cited

Adorno, Theodor (1978). *Minima Moralia: Reflections from Damaged Life*, trans. E.F.N. Jephcott. London: Verso.

Agamben, Giorgio (2000). *Means without End: Notes on Politics*, trans. Vincenzo Binetti and Cesare Casarino. Minneapolis: University of Minnesota Press.

Alperowitsch, Eduard. »Universität u. Nationalstaat«, 2. April 1948, private collection.

Arendt, Hannah (1973). *The Origins of Totalitarianism* . New York: Harcourt, Brace and Company.

Balinsky, B.I. (1982). The UNRRA University in Munich, 1945–1947«, unpublished manuscript.

Bammer, Angelika (ed.). (1994). *Displacements: Cultural Identities in Question*. Bloomington/IN: Indiana University Press.

Brodzki, Bella and Jeremy Varon (2005). The Munich Years: The Jewish Students of Post-War Germany. In Johannes-Dieter Steinert and Inge Weber-Newth (eds.). *Beyond Camps and Forced Labour: Current International Research on Survivors of Nazi Persecution. Proceedings of the First International Multidisciplinary Conference at the Imperial War Museum* (London: 29–31 January 2003). Osnabrück: Secolo.

Clifford, James (1992). Traveling Cultures. In Lawrence Grossberg, Cary Nelson and Paula A. Treichler (eds.). *Cultural Studies*, 96–116. New York: Routledge.

Gupta, Akhil and James Ferguson (eds.). (1997). *Culture, Power, Place: Explorations in Critical Anthropology*. Durham/NC: Duke University Press.

Jacobmeyer, Wolfgang (1985). *Vom Zwangsarbeiter zum Heimatlosen Ausländer. Die Displaced Persons in Westdeutschland 1945–1951*. Göttingen: Vandenhoeck & Ruprecht.

Lavie, Smadar and Ted Swedenburg (eds.). (1996). *Displacement, Diaspora, and Geographies of Identity*. Durham/NC: Duke University Press.

Malkki, Liisa (1992). National Geographic: The Rooting of Peoples and the Territorialization of Identity Among Scholars and Refugees. *Cultural Anthropology*, 7:1, 24–44.

Malkki, Liisa (1994). Citizens of Humanity: Internationalism and the Imagined Community of Nations. *Diaspora*, 3:1, 41–68.

Malkki, Liisa (1995). *Purity and Exile: Violence, Memory and National Cosmology among Hutu Refugees in Tanzania*. Chicago: University of Chicago Press.

Michelson, Valerius. Interview by David Boder, 24 September 1946, http://voices.iit.edu/interviews/miche_t.html (accessed 24 July 2001).

Novikov, M.M. (1952). *Ot Moskvy do N'iu-Iorka. Moia zhizn' v nauke i politike*. New York: Izdatel'stvo imeni Chekhova.

Ong, Aihwa (1999). *Flexibile Citizenship: The Cultural Logics of Transnationality*. Durham/NC: Duke University Press.

Pawlow, Boris (1985). Das kurze Dasein der internationalen UNRRA-Universität. Aus den Erinnerungen eines D.P. *Kontinent: Ost-West-Forum*, 32, 92.

Protocol of the third congress of the Central Representation of the Ukrainian Emigration, 19–20 November 1949, Ukrainian Free University, Fond Tsentral'ne Predstavnytstvo Ukraïns'koï Emihratsiï v Nimechchyni.

Proudfoot, Malcolm (1956). *European Refugees, 1939–52: A Study in Forced Population Movement.* Evanston/IL: Northwestern University Press

Rée, Jonathan (1992). Internationality. *Radical Philosophy*, 60, 3–11.

Tcharnobroda, Roma. Interview by David Boder, 24 September 1946, http://voices.iit.edu/interviews/tchar_t.html (accessed 24 July 2001).

Zinnemann, Fred (1992). *An Autobiography.* London: Bloomsbury.

Zittel, Bernhard (1979). Die UNRRA-Universität in München, 1945–1947. *Archivalische Zeitschrift*, 75, 281–301.

Zweig, Michael (1967). *The Idea of a World University*, ed. by Harold Taylor. Carbondale/IL: Southern Illinois University Press.

Diaspora as Possibility and Task – the Plea of a German-Jewish Woman

Kirsten Heinsohn

In June 1934, the cultural periodical *Der Morgen* published an issue devoted to the theme of »Diaspora as Task«. Its editor was Eva Reichmann-Jungmann, a well-known representative of the *Central Association of German Citizens of the Jewish Faith*, the *Centralverein*, in Berlin. The name of the association, founded in 1893, also embodied its central program. The CV, as the organisation was popularly known, fought against the anti-Semitic movement and forcefully stressed that its own members were Germans. Actually this was a matter of course, a self-evident civil fact at the time: because the majority of the Jews living in the German Reich belonged to one of the constituent German states and thus the Reich. When it came to the question of their civil status, their religious affiliation played no role. Nonetheless, since the end of the nineteenth century, there had been a widespread tendency to juxtapose »Germans« over against »Jews«. An anti-Semitic movement had successfully spread this perspective in Germany and had made it omnipresent in the public sphere. It had thus generated a discursive pattern which maintained that the two groups, defined as separate *Völker*, i.e. »peoples«, were alien to one another, antipodal and ultimately incompatible. The CV struggled vigorously against this discursive exclusion of Jews from the collective of the »Germans«; it also initiated legal steps against anti-Semitic slurs and vilification. Already from the turn of the century on, and with heightened intensity after experiences during the First World War, the CV strove to strengthen Jewish self-esteem and self-confidence. (Barnai 2002).

The periodical *Der Morgen* offered Jewish and non-Jewish intellectuals a dynamic forum for spirited discussion of issues of the day. The philosopher Julius Goldstein (1873–1929), likewise an engaged member of the CV, had founded the journal in 1925, with the aim of providing a platform for highlighting Jewish contributions to and participation in contemporary culture, giving special attention to the role of religion. It also sought to make an intellectual contribution to the fight against anti-Semitism (Fraiman 2000, 42–3). Almost every issue of the journal contained articles that actively confronted racial models of thinking. Prominent rabbis and well-known scholars, such as Franz Rosenzweig, Ernst Cassirer and Leo Baeck, published in its pages. This ambitious cultural magazine quickly acquired an excellent reputation.

At the beginning of the 1930s, a turn became evident in the journal's content, expressing a renewed sense of Jewish self-assurance. This can be seen both as a reaction to the growing Nazi movement and an active confrontation with Zionism. From October 1933, the literary scholar Hans Bach (1902–1977) and Eva Reichmann-Jungmann took over as the journal's chief editors. They turned it into a monthly and opened up the spectrum of topics dealt with. Thus, for example, *Der Morgen* also featured articles on economic questions.

When the special issue »Diaspora as Task« appeared, the juxtaposition in discourse of »Jews« and »Germans« had already been elevated to official government policy. The National Socialists had been in power for over a year and had already demonstrated in the spring of 1933, promulgating the first laws on Jews and organizing a nation-wide anti-Jewish boycott, that the new rulers had no compunctions about forging a boundary of differentiation in German society based on racial criteria. They then proceeded to impose on the groups so constructed their own special legal regulations and restrictions. For that reason, the CV, already in 1933, had begun to talk about the need for a »new emancipation«, as it searched desperately for a *modus vivendi* with the regime which would allow them to live in a modicum of dignity (Barnai 2000, 324–30).

Once again, the topic of diaspora had become timely and contemporary. During the Weimar Republic, it had not been dealt with at much length either in *Der Morgen* or in other periodicals published by Jewish Germans. The members of the CV certainly did not view themselves as a diasporic community – rather, as already mentioned, they regarded themselves as Germans with a Jewish identity.

This article first sketches at length Eva Reichmann's biography, looking at several of her writings, and some of her key experiences. In analyzing these materials, it seeks to discover what significance the concept of diaspora as a task acquired for Jewish Germans after 1933. It then goes on to explore a renewed critical confrontation with the concept after the Second World War and the establishment of the state of Israel in 1948. I will show that Reichmann's positive evaluation of the Jewish Diaspora arose directly from her experience and her critical reflection on nationalism, and she came to espouse a position arguing for a cosmopolitan »citizen-of-the world« *weltanschauung*. The plea for such an outlook was already partially present in her writings in the 1920s and early '30s, but it was not fully developed until the mid-1930s and the post-war period. It combined her personal experience, political convictions, scholarly topics and her own religious needs in mutual dynamic interaction.

Eva Reichmann (1897–1998)

In Eva Gabriele Reichmann's long life, the experience of being a Jewish woman played a central formative role, extending even to her professional activity. Eva Gabriele was born in Lublinitz (now Lubliniec/Poland) in Silesia, the youngest daughter of Agnes and Adolf Jungmann. She grew up in an acculturated yet religious parental home. Her father was an actively engaged liberal attorney, and at home the family's life was marked by what Eva Reichmann described as a »strong Jewish tradition« (Reichmann 1989, 313). Eva's family moved to Oppeln and she was especially impressed by the rabbi of the Jewish community there, Leo Baeck (1873–1956), with whom the family members were close friends. For the young Eva, then just eight years old, Baeck's departure from home town Oppeln in 1905 was a key turning point in her life. She later tried to »work through« this experience in the form of a secret »fan's collection« of all her memories of Rabbi Baeck (Reichmann 1968, 258–259). Throughout her life, she felt closely bound to Baeck personally and in terms of religion, and admired him as a veritable »symbol of German Jewry« (Reichmann 1959).

After studying economics in Breslau, Berlin and Munich, and for a time under Emil Lederer in Heidelberg, she completed a PhD at Heidelberg University in 1921 with a thesis on »Spontaneity and Ideology as a Factor in Modern Social Movements«. In 1924, Eva Jungmann entered the CV in Berlin as an expert on cultural policy. She initially had a somewhat sceptical attitude toward the CV. She saw herself at this point as a religious Jew with strong »Zionist leanings« and she actively espoused the building up of Palestine as a Jewish national home (Reichmann 1989, 317; Paucker 1997, 280). By contrast, the CV had been established to defend the civil rights of

Jews in their native homeland Germany. There was a regulation in the CV bylaws in keeping with this, stating that only German citizens could become members. The majority of the East European Jews who had migrated into Germany were thus excluded from possible membership.

Eva Jungmann expressly criticised this point in her job interview with the CV. But since the leadership echelon of the association assured her she could express her views openly, she decided to accept the offer of the CV and join its staff. From that juncture on, her activity in and for the CV put its distinctive mark on her subsequent life. She wrote that this step had »sealed her fate« (Reichmann 1989, 317). She performed her job with great loyalty and growing conviction, and saw herself as a go-between bridging between Zionists and non-Zionists, so that she quickly rose to become one of the central personalities in the CV in Berlin. Since she worked mainly on cultural and internal Jewish topics, from 1933 on as an editor of *Der Morgen*, the contradiction with her pro-Zionist »inclinations« was minimal. For example, she was a member of the *Keren Hajessod*, a society founded in 1921 to finance agricultural settlement in Palestine. It was expressly intended to organise both non-Zionists and Zionists (Brenner 2002, 96). In 1939, the *Palestine Office* in Berlin certified that she belonged »to that circle of non-Zionists who were very closely associated with the idea of the construction of Palestine and work for furthering that idea«,[1] and the leadership of the CV also gave her an excellent reference.

At the CV, she met Hans Reichmann (1900–1964), whom she married in 1930. Reichmann, a barrister, headed the CV section on combating National Socialism. From the beginning of the 1930s on, the legal work of the CV in the struggle against anti-Semitism – its primary task – evolved ever more into a political confrontation with the rising tide of National Socialism. Eva Reichmann was also involved in this political struggle, for example in a dispute in print with an ardent supporter of the NSDAP (Centralverein 1930). In subsequent decades, her later scholarly work was shaped by questions such as why the majority of Germans supported the National Socialists, and what role anti-Semitism played. From 1933 to 1938, she was active in a leadership role in several organisations in Berlin that sought to promote a positive sense of community, including the *Kul-*

1 Leo Baeck Institute/Jüdisches Museum Berlin (LBIJMB) Eva Reichmann Collection AR 904/MF 915, Box 1, Folder 1: Letter of recommendation from Benno Cohn, Palästina-Amt Berlin 24 February 1939; Letter of reference, Board of Directors, 31 December 1938.

turbund (Jewish Cultural League) and the *Jüdisches Lehrhaus* (House of Jewish Learning).

After the Novemberpogrom of 1938, Hans Reichmann was imprisoned for several weeks in the concentration camp Sachsenhausen (Reichmann 1998). Following his release, the couple fled in early 1939 via the Netherlands to London. Both remained in Great Britain after the war and in 1945 became British citizens. Initially they were still dependent for support on Jewish relief organisations, but after the end of the war both Hans and Eva Reichmann were able to build up a new career in London. Eva Reichmann completed a second doctorate at the London School of Economics in 1945, submitting a thesis on »The Social Sources of National Socialist Anti-Semitism«. It was published in 1950 as *Hostages of Civilisation*, and became her *opus magnum*, in which she combined a sociological-historical analysis of anti-Semitism with ideas from Freudian psychoanalysis (Reichmann 1950; 1956). Eva Reichmann attributed the success of National Socialism to political, social and economic upheaval in Germany after the First World War, whose potential had not become virulent until the »liberation of the instincts«, i.e. the flight into Jew-hatred by those who felt socially and politically *déclassé*. Her analysis was based in part on the works of the »Frankfurt school« in exile around Theodore Adorno and Max Horkheimer, especially their work on the authoritarian personality. Like the exponents of critical theory, Reichmann also dealt with the difficulties people encountered to find a proper orientation in modern democratic societies that were undergoing swift and profound change. She wrote that democracy was a »difficult« ideology and a demanding form of the state which placed high requirements on the »sense of justice and powers of reasoning« of the citizens. (Reichmann 1950, 110).

Until 1959, Eva Reichmann worked as director of research at the *Wiener Library* in London. Down to the present day, this library collects source material and literature on the persecution and murder of the European Jews. Eva Reichmann evaluated the files of the Nuremberg trials, building up an extensive collection of reports by contemporaries (Barkow 1997; Dalby 2007, 121–5). Both Hans and Eva Reichmann were very active in the *Society for Jewish Studies*, the *Leo Baeck Institute* (LBI), founded in 1955 (Hoffmann 2005) and the *Association of Jewish Refugees* in London. After retirement, Eva Reichmann continued to work as a lecturer and writer, especially in the *Society for Christian-Jewish Cooperation*. In this context she gave lectures in Germany, outstanding among which were her addresses at the Protestant church congresses in 1963 and 1967. In the 1960s and 1970s, she published two further studies on the sociology of the Germans and the Jews (Reichmann 1965, 1971). Only after her husband suddenly passed away in 1964 was she appointed a board member in his place in the LBI London (Nattermann 2004, 184). In 1970, she was awarded the *Buber-Rosenzweig Medal* of the *Coordination Council of the Societies for Christian-Jewish Cooperation*. In 1971, the West German government awarded her the *Federal Cross of Merit*, in 1982 the *Moses Mendelssohn Prize* of the state of Berlin, and in 1983 the highest civilian honour in West Germany, the *Great Federal Cross of Merit*. After the honours bestowed upon her in the 1980s, life became quieter for Eva Reichmann, now well over 80 years old. In September 1998, she died at the age of 101. Upon learning of her passing, the German ambassador in London Gebhardt von Moltke issued a special statement in which he acknowledged her work of reconciliation.

It is difficult to pigeonhole Eva Reichmann politically and in terms of world view. She saw herself more as a socialist scholar, raised in a liberal home, and for that reason she also maintained a positive relation to liberalism. But Eva also espoused pacifist ideas and Zionist views. She maintained this openness in her thinking and actions throughout her life, though that did not deter her from taking clear positions on historical questions when she deemed that necessary. Religiously she felt a strong affinity to liberal Judaism in the sense of Leo Baeck, a religious conviction she also made a part of her active life. This aspect of her identity was never subject to discussion, but the question where Jews should stand after 1933 in the German Reich was, as long as they had an option.

Diaspora as Task

In June 1934, in her editorial introducing the special issue of *Der Morgen* on diaspora, Eva Reichmann made it very clear that she believed the »national revolution in 1933« had brought about an »intellectual upheaval throughout Jewry« across the globe (Reichmann 1934, 97). This upheaval, namely the revocation of the emancipation of the Jews in Germany and the associated »intellectual shock«, was necessarily awakening »profound suspicions about existence in the Diaspora«. If in a country that had been considered a paragon of successful integration, the emancipation of the Jews could be nullified so swiftly, then she reasoned that Jews everywhere in the world were affected by this dark turn. It was precisely the events in 1933 which had once again made questionable the fact of Jewish dispersion »after centuries of legitimacy«. It was possible to discern a »genuine revolutionary turn of Jewish intellect and spirit«, a »longing for salvation« and a »longing for security from further crashes« (ibid.).

She noted that the Zionist idea, namely the building up of a Jewish national homeland in Palestine, had acquired a new quality compared with earlier decades. Despite her own positive attitude toward Zionism, she immediately declared that this quality was deceptive, since it was grounded on despair and »mundane bourgeois hope«, and was prepared to lightly discard insights that had organically evolved over time. On the one hand, Reichmann in this way, albeit indirectly, expressed her understanding for the hope for security by means of Zionist construction in Palestine. On the other, she articulated a clear plea: the meaning and task of the Jewish Diaspora had once more to be understood in a positive light in order to legitimate the diaspora itself. She did not wish, with little forethought, to open up the evolved organic bond between Jews and their countries of origin for critical reconsideration. Her main argument spelled this out clearly:

> »The danger is that the [Jewish ingathering and return, K. H.] are taking place in the sign of a time whose external course of events – the violent separation and removal of Jews from their homelands, and whose internal meaning – the dominance of the idea of nationalism – are all too favourable for it. All of us, now returning once again down a difficult path to our own God from the deification of an era – have reason to make sure we do not once more fall total prey to the spirit of these times, in the process sacrificing to them our own-most, our eternal [being]« (ibid., 98).

In her view diaspora was to countervail an exaggerated nationalism. By nationalism, she meant not only the prevailing German upsurge, but also Jewish, Zionist nationalism. Reichmann argued that the diaspora (in Germany) should continue to be part of a Jewish pathway in history, and thus a central Jewish task. In her eyes, exclusive concentration on building a national home in Palestine was false, and not in keeping with the singular particularity of Jewish history. She viewed Zionism as a dangerous ideology when it postulated a pure Jewish nationalism.

In another text, she developed this idea more thoroughly. It became clear that Reichmann regarded the intellectual power of Judaism as a source of benefit for the various home countries of the Jews. She rejected the »claim to totality« of Zionism, especially in its Revisionist current, which »brushes aside any other Jewish view, disparaging it as non-Jewish, inferior, devoid of character« (Reichmann 1974 [1934], 53). She also thought that the »abnormal occupational structure« of the Jews in the European countries had its quite positive sides as well, because as a result of this, a certain intellectual substance had been preserved (ibid., 55). Eva Reichmann feared that concentrating all Jewish energy on the work of settlement and construction in Palestine could bring about a »fateful change«, because the creation of a nation-state was subject to the laws of power politics. She wrote that the

> »idea of nationalism, even if espoused by a portion of its Jewish adherents in a highly purified form, is inherently subject to its own laws, which press out very consciously from the sphere of the idea into that of everyday struggle over power politics. You cannot with impunity shift from a form of existence that is purely in the realm of thought to one anchored in reality. Reality discards the purest will for shaping something new, rushing toward an existence more appropriate to it, laden with the trappings of power and guilt« (ibid., 56).

From this analysis, Eva Reichmann even concluded that the Zionist Revisionists, whose only guideline was the »nationalistic idea«, had in effect forfeited their Jewishness. This statement was clear and provocative, but also marked out the boundaries within which Eva Reichmann's Zionist sentiments were at home: she warmly accepted Zionism as an intellectual challenge, and wished those immigrating to Palestine much luck. But in 1934, Eva unmistakably rejected the idea of the establishment of a Jewish state. And this article should also be regarded as reflective of official CV opinion at the time, because it was an editorial entitled »On the Meaning of German-Jewish Existence«, published in the *CV-Zeitung* in May 1934.

So the internal Jewish fronts acted to refurbish their discursive fortifications: Eva Reichmann's positive understanding of the Jewish dispersion clashed with large segments of Zionist discourse of the day. In mainstream Zionist thought, the Diaspora was the negative antipode to the Jewish nation. It was considered a deformation of Jewish existence, because the European Jews had lost their substance and singular distinctiveness as a result of assimilation and conversion. The Zionist propagandists contrasted the physically weak »Galut Jew«, lost in lofty realms of the spirit, and living akin to a parasite, with the »new Hebrew«, a pioneer engaged in the rigors of manual labour. This »new Hebrew« pioneer actively defended the land that had been conquered, spoke Hebrew as mother tongue, and dedicated his whole life actively to the construction of the Jewish state (Schweid 1996).

Over against this interpretation, Eva Reichmann pleaded for a positive view of the diaspora as a possible »Jewish path«. In her eyes, the diaspora was not part of the feared decline and fall of Judaism, or some form of divine punishment or forced exile, but rather part of the intellectual-spiritual path in the world, and thus a special Jewish task and challenge.

Space of Experience, Horizon of Expectation

In view of the political upheavals in the German Reich after January 1933, a clear rejection of the diaspora on the part of German Jews would not have been surprising. It was specifically the Zionists who could feel that their world view had been vindicated by events: persecution of the Jews was possible again and again everywhere and the only defence was the building of a Jewish state. But the resolute »German citizens of the Jewish faith« were unable to so quickly forget the experience of past decades, and had difficulties imagining a future for them in Palestine. Hence, the intellectual defence of the diaspora and its conception as a legitimate *bona fide* »Jewish path« was also a defence of their own »space of experience« and its associated »horizon of expectation« (Koselleck 1976). The space of experience is defined as a »past that is present, whose events have been incorporated and can be recalled« (ibid., 354/355). This complex also contains non-personal experiences passed on over generations or handed down through institutions and conscious and unconscious emotional processing of events. In its dynamic interaction, experiences from the past are linked with those from the present in the space of experience.

The future, as the third temporal form of history, comes into play as a »horizon of expectation«. It signifies the »future made present« which can be developed from the space of experience. That horizon of expectation contains »hopes, fears and wishes, force of human will, concern, but also rational analysis, receptive outlook or curiosity« (ibid.). In reference to German Jewry at the beginning of the 1930s, we can assume that the positive experience over more than a century of a step-wise emancipation and integration, moving ever forward, along with a process of bourgeois acculturation among the greater segment of the Jewish minority in Germany, constituted a central core in their space of experience. Problems and frictions arose in view of the negative experience of anti-Semitic propaganda and violence, and the rising tide of social exclusion from 1933 on. The various internal Jewish groups were thus forced in the early years of the National Socialist regime to rethink their own identity and stance, both over against other internal Jewish groups, and also as declaration *vis-à-vis* the measures of the German government. In the early 1930s, the life of German Jews was marked by deepening insecurity and anxiety about the future. It was no longer clear whether past experience could be used as a guideline for action, or whether they were facing a totally new situation, for which there was as yet no store of accumulated experience.

In this context, Zionism took on a special meaning. Since its emergence in Western Europe, it had initially been a small beacon on the horizon of expectation, especially in Germany. The *Zionist Association in Germany* (ZVfD) boasted some 33,000 members by the mid-1920s, yet from that peak membership had rapidly dwindled to but 7,500 by 1930. Only beginning in 1933 did the membership clearly climb once more, reaching in excess of 20,000, although by that point in time a large number of Zionists had already emigrated (Zimmermann 1997, 30). This attraction to the Zionist ranks is a clear indicator of a change in the attitude of expectation of the approximately half a million German Jews, even if the Zionists remained a small minority. One proof of this, for example, is that from 1934 on, the paper *Israelitisches Familienblatt* – which was open to all Jewish groups and currents – published numerous positive articles on the Zionist alternative in Palestine. This paper, in an intensive critical debate with the program of the CV, sought to create a triad: the slogan was »German culture – Jewish intellectual treasures – Palestinian reality« (Zu neuen Ufern 1934).

In the 1930s, Eva Reichmann also engaged in renewed critical reflection on realities in Palestine – and once again defended the diaspora, even if her enthusiasm for building up the *Yishuv* had clearly intensified. In August 1933, she published an official »Position on Palestine« for the CV (Reichmann 1933, 311). Contrary to earlier, in part strongly-worded frontline positions, the CV now reached out to strike a chord of reconciliation, stating it was necessary to understand that both the construction of Palestine and the »securing of life for the German Jews in Germany« were part of a central common task. The consolation provided by the existence of Jewish development work in Palestine was, in her view, closely bound up with the demand incumbent on each and every Jew to actively support this work of construction. And at the same time, all were likewise called upon to solve the »German Jewish question« in Germany as well. She noted that for these two tasks to succeed, more was required than mere mutual tolerance. Both sides had to recognise one another in their essential value for maintaining Jewish life.

The more threatening the exclusion and persecution of the Jews in Germany became, the more the two camps actually joined hands and worked together. At the latest after the promulgation of the *Reichsbürgergesetz* (Reich Citizen Law) in 1935, which denied Jews the privileged status of a citizen in the new Germany, it was also evident to the CV leaders that there was no longer any hope for a »new emancipation«, for example in the form of a protective law for the collective. In the *CV-Zeitung*, there was a manifest rise in the number of articles on construction work in Palestine. A special supplement was introduced, the »Palestine Review«. But there were also ever more reports about emigration to other European countries or overseas. In October 1937, Eva Reichmann took part in a study trip to Palestine organised by the *United Jewish Cultural Leagues* and the *Berlin Zionist Association*. She reported on this trip in four articles in the *CV-Zeitung* (Reichmann 1937). Her impressions were largely positive: she praised the achievements of Jewish settlement and construction, was very impressed by the scenic beauty of the country and the determination of settlers there to work to develop it. Although these travel reports were marked by a strong emotional tenor, her final article was more distanced and circumspect: she stressed that Palestine could only absorb a fraction of persons now seeking a new Jewish home. Aside from that, the economic problems, the political confrontation over the future of the country and the violent clashes with the indigenous Arab population represented a great burden and challenge – which not all emigrants could be equal to.

Nonetheless, she felt the achievement in Palestine was truly impressive – an accomplishment all Jews could be proud of, binding them closely to Palestine. But since Palestine was not »at rest« but rather in flux, the diaspora in her view still had an important function: (a) to maintain Judaism and the Jews, and (b) to provide support to construction in the *Yishuv*. Existence in the diaspora was »necessary«, as a »value in its own right«, and »perhaps some day as a place of retreat, should the storm of history sweep even more violently across that narrow coastal strip« (Reichmann 1937 I, 2).

Even in the already intensified threat of the dire situation developing in Germany in 1937, Reichmann still defended the necessity and specific Jewish task of the diaspora. Though she recognised the central value of the Zionist path for world Jewry, she continued to criticise its associated claim to absolute and exclusive validity. As before, she argued that there were two guiding ideas in Judaism, quite apart from the concrete events of history: on the one hand, the idea of constructing »Jewish life in the land of the fathers«, on the other, the idea to shape and nurture »Jewish life in the broader world, organically« (Berichte und Referate 1936).

Eva Reichmann felt a strong personal attachment and obligation to that second idea. She wished to remain in Germany and continue to carry out her »Jewish task« there. Before her husband was arrested and interned in Sachsenhausen in November 1938, she had not considered emigration. But Hans Reichmann was only released after his wife could present a visa for a departure to the United States. The couple was initially convinced that they would later be able to return, but decided against that when they became aware of the extent of the violence against Jews being perpetrated by the German regime.

Jewish Diaspora after 1945: New Reasons and Rationale

Neither her awareness of the Shoah nor the establishment of the state of Israel could dissuade Eva Reichmann from continuing to view the diaspora as an important core principle of Jewish existence. Along with this conviction, which she had already articulated in the 1930s, after 1945 a second argument entered the picture: She also espoused the idea of diaspora to bolster her interpretation of the history of the Jews in Germany, grounded on a positive evaluation of emancipation. By contrast, Zionist writers such as Gershom Scholem maintained that emancipation had been a pure illusion and that there had never been a serious »German-Jewish dialogue« (Scholem 1964; 1965). That is a dictum often repeated, right down to the present.

But even as a person in exile, Eva Reichmann did not wish to see her Germanness, her native *Deutschtum* and that of the German Jews questioned. In addition, she did not regard the establishment of the Israeli state as a final solution to the »Jewish question«. In 1974, she wrote that it was important »to show once again the Jewish-historical legitimacy of the Diaspora« (Reichmann 1974, 280/281). In an essay in 1980, she called the world-wide Jewish Diaspora and the state of Israel the two »focal points«, both important and necessary for Jewish identification, just as these had before 1933 been the two poles of »German-Jewish existence« (Reichmann 1980). In her legitimation of the Jewish Diaspora, Eva Reichmann added two new viewpoints: (a) the necessity to preserve (German) Liberal (Reform) Judaism and (b) the demand that events in Germany between 1933 and 1945 should not be seen as a »final verdict of history« on Jewish existence in diaspora.

With these two points, Eva Reichmann, as a German-Jewish woman, also defended in critical reflection her own »space of experience« against any subsequent devaluation, although return to Germany for her was now out of the question. She had built up a secure professional life for herself in London. In Germany after the destruction of all Jewish organisations, there was no longer any post to which she might have been able to return. Moreover, after 1945 it was only possible for her to live as a Reform Jew outside Germany, because all the new Jewish congregations in the Federal Republic were Orthodox. In 1939, a Reform German-Jewish congregation had been established in London, which formed a separate department inside the *English Liberal Synagogue*: it was called the *New Liberal Jewish Congregation at Belsize Square Synagogue* (Godfrey 2005). In the *Belsize Congregation*, services followed the Reform rite practiced in Berlin and Frankfurt am Main in the 1920s; down to the early 1960s, these services were even held in German (Berghahn 1984/1988, 167–72). Likewise in the Leo Baeck Lodge, a sub-group of the *B'nai B'rith* in England set up in 1943; those active were exclusively German-Jewish emigrants. Both groups emphasised the special role of culture in Judaism. Eva Reichmann was a member of the *Belsize Congregation* and other institutions of the group of German-Jewish emigrants, where she had found a new »home«, both socially and in terms of religion.

In this regard, Eva Reichmann was not the exception, but rather the rule. It is precisely religious identification that often played a central role (and still does) for group cohesion and individual self-assessment in groups in the diaspora – possibly even a stronger role than in the country of origin. Thus, for example, German-Jewish emigrants in England, and their children, were not clear about where they should stand when it came to questions of nationality in Great Britain, but they were all very certain they were Jews (Berghahn 1984). Eva Reichmann's assertion that a vital diaspora could fortify Judaism finds here a certain confirmation.

It was precisely the *space of exile* that offered German Jews several possibilities for religious identification. In the Federal Republic or in parts of Israel, they were not compelled to conform to the laws of religious Orthodoxy in order to live in harmony with their religious needs and convictions. In this manner a diaspora in a positive sense could crystallise from the midst of exile – one in which religion was characterised by pluralism and its own inherent spiritual and ethical value. In diaspora, it would probably be more possible to harmonise shattered national identifications and positive Jewish self-definition and to create continuity, at least for oneself.

If exile in this way was a pillar of support for Reform Judaism, in the case of many it also led to a fruitful confrontation with their own feelings of nationalism. This had been the case with Eva Reichmann as well. Theoretically, she had always had a critical approach to nationalism of any stripe, but emotionally she felt a strong bond with the essential »German character«. In an interview in 1989, she commented on that attitude, saying that she was herself very conscious of the shallowness of the »German feeling of nationalism«. It had always »easily slid off into something pathological«, and as long as she was still in Germany, she had been an »assiduous participant«. Her exile in London had finally opened her eyes to this. For that reason, she stated, she also viewed her time in exile as some sort of »compensation« for the injustice which her family had experienced, because in the process she had come to know »two peoples from the inside out« (Reichmann 1989, 328).

The second point of view formed a central component in her writings and speeches after 1945. She defended the history and emancipation of the Jews in Germany. In her view, events after 1933 were no proof for the hypothesis that the idea of emancipation as such – and thus also the diaspora – had failed. In an after-word to a new edition of several of her essays, she wrote in 1974:

»Despite our foundering on the rocks of place and time, we sustained our belief that the authority of the human rights which the historical era that was so forcibly terminated had introduced had not been extinguished with its demise. We grasped our precipitous fall as a fate deeply anchored in the nature and history of the surrounding German world. And precisely for that reason it was not some sort of inevitable law of development assigned to Jewish diasporic existence under other spatial and temporal conditions. We had experienced Jewish Diaspora in all its fertility and danger. We were mindful of its achievements, very especially in Germany. And we recognized that Diaspora would continue to exist along side the rebirth of a Jewish national home.« (Reichmann 1974, 281)

It was her goal to lift up the »internal Jewish dispute [...] into a melodious harmony for several voices« (ibid., 282), i.e. to combine her own benevolent accompaniment of Zionism with the changing history of the »German-Jewish path« without elevating one of the two sides to an absolute.

Eva Reichmann's impassioned plea for the diaspora as an important positive principle of Jewish existence also served at the same time as a defence of German-Jewish history and her own life trajectory. Only in the ambit of the diaspora was she able to reconcile and harmonise her own identifications with political and religious convictions. Her thoughts and actions were marked in particular by openness and an abiding recognition of those who thought differently. Though she spoke as a German-Jewish woman, she associated this with a universal intellectual attitude that can be termed »cosmopolitan«. A modern »cosmopolitan outlook« (Ulrich Beck) was already present in her writings. That outlook rendered the »recognition of Otherness« a »maxim in thought, in life together, and in action«. Differences perceived are neither ordered in a hierarchy nor dissolved. Rather, they are consciously accepted and viewed as positive (Beck/Grande 2004, 27; Nussbaum 1996). Cosmopolitan thinking is thus not antagonistic to the nation and nationalism, but it demands that that these aspects be viewed as constituting but one *part* of patterns shaping the way human beings identify with broader structures – rather than something that is deemed absolute *vis-à-vis* other elements (Kaldor 1996).

Eva Reichmann's recommendations for embracing the diaspora as a Jewish task and possibility were grounded precisely on this conviction. She retained her cosmopolitan openness even in difficult personal and political times. Though she adapted her rationale and arguments for Jewish diasporic existence to the new realities, she changed nothing in her fundamental convictions. The further development of the relations between the state of Israel and the Jewish communities in diaspora down to the present day would seem to confirm her analysis: both sides, despite various problems one with the other, are still mutually and dynamically interdependent (Sheffer 2002; Gold 2004).

Translated by Bill Templer

Works cited

Barkai, Avraham (2002). *»Wehr Dich!«: Der Centralverein deutscher Staatsbürger jüdischen Glaubens (C.V.) 1893–1938.* Munich: C. H. Beck.

Barkow, Ben (1997). *Alfred Wiener and the Making of the Holocaust Library.* London: Vallentine Mitchell.

Beck, Ulrich (2004). *Der kosmopolitische Blick, oder: Krieg ist Frieden.* Frankfurt/Main.: Suhrkamp.

Beck, Ulrich and Edgar Grande (2004). *Das kosmopolitische Europa. Gesellschaft und Politik in der Zweiten Moderne.* Frankfurt/Main: Suhrkamp.

Berghahn, Marion (1984). *Continental Britons. German-Jewish Refugees from Nazi Germany.* New York, Oxford: Berghahn.

Berichte und Referate (1936). Organisches und Organisiertes Judentum. *Berliner Gemeindeblatt 24. Mai.*

Brenner, Michael (2002). *Geschichte des Zionismus.* Munich: C.H. Beck.

Centralverein deutscher Staatsbürger jüdischen Glaubens (1930). *Eine Aussprache über die Judenfrage zwischen Margarete Adam und Eva Reichmann-Jungmann;* mit einem Nachwort: Warum habe ich nationalsozialistisch gewählt? Berlin: CV-Verlag.

Dalby, Hannah-Vilette (2007). German-Jewish Female Intellectuals and the Recovery of German-Jewish Heritage in the 1940s and 1950s. *Leo Baeck Institute Yearbook*, LII, 111–28.

Fraiman, Sarah (2000). The Transformation of Jewish Consciousness in Nazi Germany as reflected in the German Jewish Journal »Der Morgen«, 1925–1938. *Modern Judaism*, 20:1, 41–59.

Godfrey, Antony (2005). *Three Rabbis in a Vicarage. The Story of Belsize Square Synagogue.* London: Larsen Grove Press.

Gold, Steven J. (2004). From Nationality to Peoplehood: Adaptation and Identity Formation in the Israeli Diaspora. *Diaspora*, 13:2/3, 331–58.

Hoffmann, Christhard (ed.). (2005). *Preserving the Legacy of German Jewry. A History of the Leo Baeck Institute, 1955–2005.* Tübingen: Mohr Siebeck.

Kaldor, Mary (1996). Cosmopolitanism versus Nationalism: The New Divide? In Richard Caplan and John Feffer (eds.). *Europe's New Nationalism. States and Minorities in Conflict*, 42–58. Oxford University Press.

Koselleck, Reinhart (1979). »Erfahrungsraum« und »Erwartungshorizont« – zwei historische Kategorien. In Reinhard Koselleck. *Vergangene Zukunft. Zur Semantik vergangener Zeiten*, 349–375. Frankfurt/Main: Suhrkamp.

Nattermann, Ruth (2004). *Deutsch-Jüdische Geschichtsschreibung nach der Shoah. Die Gründung und Frühgeschichte des Leo Baeck Institute.* Essen: Klartext-Verlag.

Nussbaum, Martha C. (1996). Patriotism and Cosmopolitanism. In Martha C. Nussbaum and Joshua Cohen (eds.). *For love of Country: Debating the Limits of Patriotism*, 3–20. Boston: Beacon Press.

Paucker, Arnold (1997). Eva Gabriele Reichmann. In Hans Erler, Ernst Ludwig Ehrlich and Ludger Heid (eds.). *»Meinetwegen ist die Welt erschaffen«. Das intellektu-*

elle Vermächtnis des deutschsprachigen Judentums. 58 Porträts, 279–284. Frankfurt/Main–New York: Campus.

Reichmann-Jungmann, Eva G. (1933). Unsere Stellung zum Palästinaproblem. *CV-Zeitung*, 3 August 1933, 317.

Reichmann-Jungmann, Eva G. (1934). Diaspora als Aufgabe. *Der Morgen*, 10:3, 97–8.

Reichmann, Eva G. (1974) [1934]. Vom Sinn deutsch-jüdischen Seins. In Eva Reichmann. *Größe und Verhängnis deutsch-jüdischer Existenz. Zeugnisse einer tragischen Begegnung*, 48–62. Heidelberg: Lambert Schneider.

Reichmann-Jungmann, Eva G. (1937). Palästinafahrt. *Palästina-Umschau der CV-Zeitung*, No. 43, 3. Beiblatt, 28 October 1937, 11–2; No. 45, 5. Beiblatt, 11 November 1937, 17–8; No.46, 4. Beiblatt, 19 November 1937, 13–4; No. 47, 4. Beiblatt, 25 November 1937, 15–6.

Reichmann-Jungmann, Eva G. (1937 I). Palästina – Idee und Wirklichkeit. *CV-Zeitung*, 49, 9 December 1937, 1–2.

Reichmann, Eva G. (1950). *Hostages of Civilisation. The Social Sources of National-Socialist Anti-Semitism.* London: Victor Gollancz.

Reichmann, Eva G. (1956). *Flucht in den Hass. Die Ursachen der deutschen Judenkatastrophe.* Frankfurt/Main.: Europäische Verlagsanstalt.

Reichmann, Eva G. (1974) [1959]. Symbol des deutschen Judentums. In Eva Reichmann. *Größe und Verhängnis deutsch-jüdischer Existenz. Zeugnisse einer tragischen Begegnung*, 267–272. Heidelberg: Lambert Schneider.

Reichmann, Eva G. (1960). The Study of Contemporary History as a Political and Moral Duty. In Max Beloff (ed.). *On the Tracks of Tyranny*, 189–200. London: Vallentine Mitchell. German Version: Zeitgeschichte als politische und moralische Aufgabe. In Eva Reichmann. *Größe und Verhängnis deutsch-jüdischer Existenz. Zeugnisse einer tragischen Begegnung*, 90–104. Heidelberg: Lambert Schneider.

Reichmann, Eva G. (1965). Diskussionen über die Judenfrage 1930–1932. In Werner E. Mosse and Arnold Paucker (eds.). *Entscheidungsjahr 1932. Zur Judenfrage in der Endphase der Weimarer Republik*, 503–53. Tübingen: Mohr Siebeck.

Reichmann, Eva G. (1974) [1968]. Die Juden in Oppeln. Kindheitserinnerungen an Rabbiner Dr. Baeck. In Eva Reichmann. *Größe und Verhängnis deutsch-jüdischer Existenz. Zeugnisse einer tragischen Begegnung*, 257–66. Heidelberg: Lambert Schneider.

Reichmann, Eva G. (1971). Der Bewußtseinswandel der deutschen Juden. In Werner E. Mosse and Arnold Paucker (eds.). *Deutsches Judentum in Krieg und Revolution 1916–1923*, 511–612. Tübingen: Mohr Siebeck.

Reichmann, Eva G. (1974). *Größe und Verhängnis deutsch-jüdischer Existenz. Zeugnisse einer tragischen Begegnung.* Heidelberg: Lambert Schneider.

Reichman, Eva G. (1980). Zwei Mittelpunkte. Juden in Israel – Juden in der Diaspora. In Gerhard Grohs (ed.). *Kulturelle Identität im Wandel. Beiträge zum Verhältnis von Bildung, Entwicklung und Religion.* Dietrich Goldschmidt zum 65. Geburtstag, 259–67. Stuttgart: Klett-Cotta.

Reichmann, Eva G. (1989). Tragt ihn mit Stolz, den gelben Fleck. In Hajo Funke (ed.). *Die andere Erinnerung. Gespräche mit jüdischen Wissenschaftlern im Exil*, 311–35. Frankfurt/Main.: Fischer.

Reichmann, Hans (1998). *Deutscher Bürger und verfolgter Jude. Novemberpogrom und KZ Sachsenhausen 1937 bis 1939.* Bearbeitung von Michael Wildt. Munich: Oldenbourg.

Scholem, Gershom (1964). Wider den Mythos vom Deutsch-Jüdischen Gespräch. *Bulletin des Leo Baeck Instituts*, 7:25–8, 278–81.

Scholem, Gershom (1965). Noch einmal: Das Deutsch-Jüdische »Gespräch«. *Bulletin des Leo Baeck Instituts*, 8:29–32, 167–72.

Schweid, Eliezer (1996). The Rejection of the Diaspora in Zionist Thought: Two Approaches. In Jehuda Reinharz and Anita Shapira (eds.). *Essential Papers on Zionism*, 133–60. New York: University Press.

Sheffer, Gabriel (2002). A Nation and Its Diaspora: A Re-examination of Israeli-Jewish Diaspora Relations. *Diaspora*, 11:3, 331–58.

Zeugen des Jahrhunderts (1982). *Eva G. Reichmann im Gespräch mit Hans Lamm.* Television Interview ZDF, 8 February 1982.

Zimmermann, Moshe (1997). *Die deutschen Juden 1914–1945.* Munich: Oldenbourg.

Zu neuen Ufern (1934). *Israelitisches Familienblatt*, 20 December 1934.

»The Song of Everyone without a Homeland«: A Palestinian Writer in »Cosmopolitan« Beirut

Kate Daniels

For millennia, the Lebanese city of Beirut has been deemed a seductive destination. Admired by Arabs and non-Arabs alike for its urbanity, intellectual openness and energy, its considerable natural beauty, its dynamic, *laissez-faire* economy and political pluralism, the Eastern Mediterranean's one-time leading *entrepôt* is also ironically notorious for its inter-sectarian and inter-communal violence, culminating most spectacularly in Lebanon's civil war of 1975–90. And yet, in spite of fifteen years of armed conflict and more recent bloody hostilities besides, the long-cherished fantasy of a cosmopolitan Beirut prevails – though, arguably, more for those outside the city than for its own inhabitants.

Is Beirut – and was it ever – a cosmopolitan city? The aim of this paper is to consider modern Beirut's claim to a cosmopolitan identity, and to assess the trajectory this cosmopolitanism has taken. It will examine the motif of Beirut's cosmopolitanism within the context of the life and career of Mahmud Darwish (1941–2008), one of the Arab world's foremost modern writers and intellectuals, acclaimed popularly as the »national poet of Palestine«. Reference will be given chiefly to three literary texts by Darwish, each of which was written in response to Israel's invasion and siege of Beirut in the summer of 1982, and the subsequent exodus of the Palestinian resistance from Lebanon. These are his epic poem *Qasidat Bayrut* (Ode to Beirut, 1984),[1] his lyric anthem *Madih al-Zill al-'Ali* (A Eulogy for the High Shadow, 1993),[2] and his extended autobiographical prose narrative *Dhakira li'l-Nisyan* (Memory for Forgetfulness, 1995),[3] an account of Hiroshima Day (6 August) during Israel's siege of the Lebanese capital. What will become evident is how Beirut's cosmopolitan character was tested by the Palestinian presence in the city, first with the wave of refu-

1 Hereafter *Ode.*

2 Hereafter *Eulogy.*

3 Hereafter *Memory.*

gees that followed the Palestinian *Nakba* (Catastrophe) of 1948, then with the second wave that followed the June War of 1967.

Beirut's Cosmopolitan History

The term »cosmopolitan« has numerous applications, relating to individuals and groups, contexts and environments, ideologies and behaviours. The city of Beirut may be identified as having been historically cosmopolitan on account of its multilingual, multicultural and multidenominational groupings; its cultural »promiscuity«; its large artistic and intellectual communities; and its location at the heart of international business and high finance (Zubeida 1999, 15–7).

Beirut emerges as a cosmopolitan centre of the late Ottoman Empire from around the nineteenth century onwards. In addition to its local Arab population, itself composed of numerous faith groups and sects, Beirut was also host to a local Jewish population, and sizeable European diplomatic, trading and religious (particularly missionary) communities, among them French, Italians, Austrians, Russians, British and North Americans. Then, as now, Beirut served as a nexus for banking and trade between Arab and non-Arab economies. In the wake of the massacres and dispersal of Armenians and Assyrians in 1914 and 1915 respectively, Beirut also became a haven for both of these communities, while also being home to small Kurdish and Persian minorities. To this day, the Arabic, French, English and Armenian languages remain in use in Lebanon, a fact that is reflected in its polyglot print media, while some 17 religious denominations are represented among its populace. Beirut may be said to have been most identifiably cosmopolitan under the *aegis* of Ottoman rule, since in the context of its imperial subjects at least, these were seen ostensibly to belong to one single community, inhabiting one open and undefined imperial territory.

Gaining its independence in 1943, the Lebanese Republic evolved as part of a broader regional struggle against western imperial domination. Hence, we witness the departure of many of Beirut's European and non-Arab elements at this time, alongside the emergence of »trends which focused on defining one's identity in opposition to Europe« (Meijer 1999, 7), such as the Islamist and local or regional nationalist movements. At this salient juncture in Beirut's history, »the deathknell of cosmopolitanism was proclaimed in the name of ›authentic‹ Arab indigenous values« (ibid., 8). Within just a few years of the Lebanese nation-state's creation, however, tensions between local and regional preoccupations came to the fore with the *Nakba*, which prompted the dispersion (*shatat*) of »between 77 and 83 percent of the Palestinians who lived in the part of Palestine that later became Israel – i.e., 78 percent of Mandatory Palestine« (Sa'di 2002, 175). By 1950, well over 100,000 Palestinian refugees had been displaced to Lebanon,[4] a number that has since grown to over 400,000 (around ten percent of Lebanon's total population).[5] Most of those dispersed to Beirut from Palestine's rural areas found shelter in makeshift, densely populated, peripheral refugee camps, while those from cities and Palestine's social elites made homes in the central Ras Beirut area.

Possibilities for co-existence in Beirut were soon tested following the influx of the Palestinians. In contrast to the positive cultural and economic commingling that had, in the main, characterised Beirut's relations with its European and other non-Arab elements, the arrival of this politically contentious, dispossessed population group, at such a critical time in Lebanon's nation building process, negatively inflected Beirut's traditional ethic of hospitality. Though the Palestinians were Arabs, and thus from a common cultural universe to the Lebanese, they were nonetheless viewed by their hosts as aliens, and for sectors of Lebanon's autochthonous population (notably isolationist Maronite Christian elements), their existence in the country was undesirable, since they were largely Sunni Muslims and thereby tilted Lebanon's delicate sectarian balance. Meanwhile, with heavily circumscribed opportunities for entry into Beirut's civic and Lebanese national life, the camp-dwelling Palestinians became increasingly aggrieved by their spatial and social exclusion from the Lebanese majority and Beirut's metropolis. The *United Nations Relief and Works Agency for Palestine Refugees in the Near East* (UNRWA) reports in 2008:

---

4 The *United Nations Relief and Works Agency for Palestine Refugees in the Near East* (UNRWA) reports in 2008 that, by 1950, it had registered 127,600 Palestinian refugees in Lebanon. It notes that registration is voluntary, and that as such their statistics are not fully representative. See http://www.un.org/unrwa/refugees/pdf/reg-ref.pdf. (accessed 28 March 2009).

5 Figures as of 30 June 2008, see http://www.un.org/unrwa/refugees/lebanon.html. (accessed 28 March 2009).

»Palestine refugees in Lebanon face specific problems. They do not have social and civil rights, and have very limited access to the government's public health or educational facilities and no access to public social services. The majority rely entirely on UNRWA as the sole provider of education, health and relief and social services. Considered as foreigners, Palestine refugees are prohibited by law from working in more than 70 trades and professions. This has led to a very high rate of unemployment amongst the refugee population«..

Cosmopolitanism in Beirut's »Golden Age«

In spite of forewarnings of cleavages rending Lebanese society, the period 1943–75 is deemed to be Beirut's »golden age« (Khalaf 2002, 153–203), and it was during this period that, »deservedly or not [...] Beirut's image as a cosmopolitan, sophisticated, polyglot meeting place of world cultures was being embellished« (ibid., 170). Accounts by Arabs and non-Arabs of everyday life in the »Paris« or »Switzerland« of the Middle East are legion. As one western commentator avers, before the civil war Beirut was a »locus of social interaction and exchange, reflecting the country's rich mix of religions, social classes, culture, tolerance and hospitality in a politically ›free‹ atmosphere« (Davie 2008, 324). Kamal Boullata (2003, 24), a Palestinian artist, also remarks:

»Beirut became a sanctuary and meeting place for political and cultural dissidents from neighbouring Arab countries […]. [Its] brand of openness created the ideal environment for becoming a microcosm of the Arab world, embracing all its distinctions and contradictions. During three eventful decades in which the region seethed with social and political upheaval, Beirut served as a lightning rod for all the political movements erupting in the Arab world since Palestine's fall.«

Beirut's cultural and intellectual life was no less vibrant and eclectic; with its many theatres, cinemas and art galleries, most of these situated in Hamra in West Beirut, the city's young, educated elites, artists, intellectuals and students consorted with international expatriates from banks, businesses and foreign cultural missions in that locality. Built in the 1950s, Hamra represented »the epitome of modernity, the ideal space to express new – and often radical – ideas, ideals and mores and to link up with the economies and cultures of Europe and the US« (Davie 2008, 318). As Boullata (2003, 24) notes, with apparent admiration: »Beirut's form of cosmopolitanism dared simultaneously to act as the crucible of Arab nationalism and to be fully open to the West.« Thus, during this golden age Lebanese poets produced texts in both Arabic and French, while local audiences enjoyed performances by foreign dance and theatre companies, alongside Arab folkloric productions and concerts by regional music stars.

As a pluralistic free haven for social, cultural and intellectual exchange, Beirut was also home to some of the Arab world's most influential avant-garde presses and publications, invariably aligned to different intellectual currents and political trends. Among these were the leftist, pan-Arab literary journal *al-Adab* (founded 1952), and *Shi'r* (founded 1957), which prioritised individualised aesthetics over ideological precedence.[6] For those Arab authors keen to avoid the excisions of the censor in their home countries or to find a printing house with the audacity to take a chance on an avant-garde publishing venture, Beirut was customarily the publishing centre of choice. An inordinately large number of the Arab world's most distinguished writers have spent periods, long or otherwise, of their literary careers in Beirut, either before or during Lebanon's war years. A non-exhaustive list includes: the Syrian Nizar Qabbani and the Syrian-Lebanese Adonis; the Lebanese Ghada al-Samman, Khalil Hawi, Yusuf al-Khal, Suhail Idris and Elias Khoury; the Iraqi Sa'di Yusuf; and the Palestinians Ghassan Kanafani, 'Izz al-Din al-Munasara, Isma'il Shammut, Mu'in Basisu and Mahmud Darwish. Amidst the coffee shops and literary salons of Hamra, refugee or exiled Palestinian artists mixed freely with locals and other expatriates, in spite of their exclusion from other areas of national life.

Mahmud Darwish: »Citizen of the World«

Mahmud Darwish (1941–2008) has assumed an almost iconic cultural and political status in the Arab world, his more than forty-year *oeuvre* constituting a lyrical chronicle of the Palestinian saga. Darwish's biography is of some interest here: with the devastation of his village in the *Nakba*, he was forced as a six-year-old child to seek refuge in Lebanon with his family. Just one year later, he returned covertly to the new Israeli state, too belatedly to be registered as an (Arab) Israeli national. Thus, Darwish's status is

6 Other Beirut-based literary journals of note include *Hiwar*, founded 1962, and *Mawaqif*, founded 1968.

described as that of an »internal refugee«, while his formative years were marked by restrictions on his movement, imprisonments and spells under house arrest. A *protégé* of the *Israeli Communist Party* (ICP), Darwish left Israel in 1970 to study political economy in the Soviet Union, relocating briefly to Cairo and then to Beirut in 1973. Here, he edited the PLO Research Centre's monthly journal *Shu'un Filistiniyya* (*Palestinian Affairs*), becoming centre director in 1975. Expelled with other PLO functionaries on Israel's 1982 occupation of Lebanon, Darwish lived later in Tunisia, London and Paris and returned to the West Bank town of Ramallah in 1995. With Israel's siege of that city in 2002, he spent extended periods in the Jordanian capital, Amman. He died in Houston, Texas, in 2008, of complications arising from his third heart operation.

Through a confluence of inescapable tragedy and design, Darwish emerges as a cosmopolitan by almost any definition. Compelled by both the exigencies of history and ideological conviction, he transmogrified into a multilingual »travelling intellectual«, having fluency in Arabic, Hebrew, French and English, thereby acquiring the universalising coloring and sensibilities of a »citizen of the world«.[7] Yet Darwish's career was distinguished, if not engendered, by his commitment to and advocacy of the Palestinian national cause; further, his was a voice that sought incontrovertibly to unify national, political and cultural specificities with universalities. His formation as part of the Communist[8] and nationalist movements of the 1950s and 1960s, his engagement with Israeli Jewish writers and artists (through ICP activities and later projects such as his literary quarterly, *al-Karmel*), his espousal of the causes of internationally deterritorialised and dispossessed humans – all this betrays an ethos that is rooted in a universalistic, humanist vision, in spite of – if not *because of* – his narrower priorities of Palestinian return and self-determination.

A secularist and freethinker, Darwish long refused to submit to the absolutes of religious authority, while pronouncing the desirability of reli-

7 A »citizen of the world« is the generic definition of a »cosmopolitan«. Along with »travelling intellectual«, »citizen of the world« appears to presuppose a degree of privilege and mobility through the possession of independent means. It should be mentioned that, though in exile, Darwish was *not* a refugee, while his international career afforded both economic and professional opportunities for mobility. Thus, Darwish is interesting, in that he presents a conflation of cosmopolitanism by both choice *and* by compulsion.

8 As he states: »The Communist party was the only party that defended the Arabs and called for coexistence between Arabs and Jews« (Darwish 2002, 72).

gious tolerance and remaining sceptical of political authority.[9] A self-proclaimed PLO »dove« (Darwish 2002, 76), Darwish has also been described as a political pragmatist, layman, and non-partisan. »I believe in pluralism«, he has stated, »I believe there is room for all religions in Palestine« (ibid., 76). Darwish's cosmopolitanism is, arguably, both cultural *and* moral, owing to his privileging of the virtues of cultural dialogue and diversity, founded on the principles of upholding human dignity, rights and justice for all, and on his keen sense of global consciousness and universal fellowship. From an early stage in his career, Darwish challenged Israeli Jewish liberal and humanist writers to interact with their Palestinian Arab compeers, and to engage with their common concerns in respect of civil rights and liberties, social change and opposition to militarism. It was partly in recognition of this that Darwish was awarded the US-based *Lannan Foundation's* 2001 *Cultural Freedom Prize*, in line with its honouring of individuals »whose extraordinary and courageous work celebrates the human right to freedom of imagination, inquiry and expression«, and for his »courage in speaking out against injustice and oppression, while eloquently arguing for a peaceful and equitable coexistence between Palestinian Arabs and Israeli Jews«.[10]

A retrospective overview of Darwish's career suggests that, as a »modest« or »moderate« cosmopolitan with transcultural and transnational interests, he saw no inherent contradiction between his engaging with the human cultural legacy in its entirety and his foregrounding of the Palestinian cultural tradition. Nor does he descend at any moment in his texts into immoderate chauvinism or exclusivist nationalist sentiment. In one small but significant respect, however, Darwish confounds the paradigm of a »citizen of the world«: exemplified by his early, indignant disavowal of his exile in his pronouncement *My homeland is not a suitcase*,[11] he seems unable ever to feel truly »at home« in his various *loci*. For him, a sense of »otherness« is constantly in evidence, while the spectre of the lost homeland and the desire for return remain constant. Further, some may make the case that Darwish's strong advocacy of Palestinian right to culture, plus his

9 Following his election to the PLO's Executive Committee in 1987, Darwish drafted the Palestinian Declaration of Independence in 1988, though he resigned and broke with the PLO in 1993, on Arafat's signing with Rabin of the Oslo Declaration of Principles.

10 http://www.lannan.org/lf/cf/detail/mahmoud-darwish-awarded-2001-cultural-freedom-award (accessed 30 March 2009).

11 From his poem *Diary of a Palestinian Wound*, written in the late 1960s. As we shall see, Darwish was later to revise this statement.

commitment to the Palestinians' right to unconditional national self-determination, are themselves irreconcilably »anti-cosmopolitan« attitudes.

Darwish defines his Beirut Experience

By the time of his arrival to Lebanon in 1973, Beirut was already an evocative *lieu de mémoire* for Darwish, patched together from remembered fragments of a visit he had made there as boy refugee. In *Memory* (86–7) he writes:

»I came to Beirut 34 years ago. I was six years old then. They put a cap on my head and left me in Al-Burj Square. It had a streetcar, and I rode the streetcar. It ran on two parallel lines made of iron. The streetcar went up I didn't know where. It ran on two iron lines. It moved forward. I couldn't tell what made this big, noisy toy move: the lines of iron laid on the ground or the wheels that rolled. I looked out the window of the streetcar. I saw many buildings and many windows, with many eyes peering out. I saw many trees. [...]

When I came back to Beirut ten years ago [...] I had come from Cairo and was searching for the small footsteps of a boy who had taken steps larger than himself, not in keeping with his age and greater than his stride. What was I searching for? The footsteps, or the boy?«

As in his childhood, Darwish's finding himself in Beirut as an adult did not come about of his own volition. For, he explains: »I had been placed under conditions [in Israel] that were no longer bearable. I had not been allowed to leave Haifa for eight years, and I had been under house arrest for three years without being told why« (Darwish 2002, 74). By contrast, the dynamic cultural milieu of Ras Beirut, in which the exiled poet now lived, placed few restrictions on his expression and literary activities. As Darwish states: »Beirut was like a platform and a workshop for dialogue. It was a city that exported books to all parts of the Arab world, and an open space for numerous and different kinds of human relationships« (Darwish, 1989). Similarly, in *Memory* (134–5) he writes: »Beirut was the place where political information and expression flourished. Beirut was the birthplace for thousands of Palestinians who knew no other cradle. Beirut was an island upon which Arab immigrants dreaming of a new world landed«.
Of Beirut's »golden age«, he recalls: »Beirut was the capital of Arab modernity [...] all cultures met there. [...] Lebanon was also a bridge between East

and West. [...] Culturally speaking, it was the center of things« (Darwish 2002, 74).

With respect to his creative process, the most significant factor to corrupt Darwish's Beirut experience was the outbreak of civil war in 1975. As he looks back, and with no little regret, he claims:

»The Beirut phase was not a decisive transition. For one simple reason: because all that tumult, all that blood and all that noise did not leave the poet much time to contemplate the conditions of poetry. Therefore, when I look at the poetry I wrote in Beirut, I can say that much of it can be crossed out« (Darwish 1998).

And yet Darwish's art could not have evolved as it did without Beirut, for it was there that he discovered that »exile exists everywhere [...] [that] exile is multicultural. It's a major theme in literature, not simply a Palestinian question« (Darwish 2002, 77). It was also in Beirut that he developed »epic lyricism«,[12] so readily adaptive to the wandering of the exile in a Mediterranean city-port founded by ancient seafarers. Hence epic lyricism as it finds its genesis in Beirut expresses »a sense of a voyage, a human voyage between cultures and peoples [...] it has a collective voice, not simply an individual one« (ibid., 69). As Darwish contemplates the tragic irony of taking the route to North Africa once traversed by his Phoenician forebears,[13] he notes how the Palestinian drama has become »the continuation of Ulysses's voyage, the sense that we have no shore, no port, that we travel from one place to another without being allowed to stay in any one place for too long« (ibid., 70).

Beirut: Exploding the Cosmopolitan Fantasy

Darwish's three Beirut texts offer representations of a polis simultaneously *remembered* as cosmopolitan yet *experienced* in contradistinction. Noticeably, its one-time networks of artists and intellectuals have dissipated during the war, and its political dissident groups have since dispersed and gone to ground. Having traded the city's once limitless horizons for a few narrow streets in Hamra, Darwish records the occasional encounter with dilet-

12 An appellation given to Darwish's longer Beirut poems by the Greek poet Yannis Ritsos.

13 On its departure from Beirut, the PLO established itself in Tunis.

tantes and *flâneurs* of various nationalities, among them numerous (unnamed) Palestinian and Lebanese writers, a Kurdish novelist, and Egyptian and Iraqi poets.[14] In *Ode*, he alludes to a snatch of literary discourse on Kafka, Rimbaud and Cavafy with a fellow poet in the Hotel Commodore. Meanwhile, *Memory* reveals how Beirut's downtown hotels have become bases for new transnational groupings, such as foreign correspondents and profiteers of all nationalities.

As the then site of the Palestinian leadership in exile, and home to one of the largest Palestinian diasporic communities, it is clear that Darwish identifies Beirut – at least in part – with the Palestinian *patria*. If, in the context of his poetry, the lost land of Palestine is the symbolic mother, Beirut in turn has become its orphaned progeny's »foster mother« (Darwish 1995, 134). And, just as the homeland is rendered in text as the foresworn sweetheart of the Palestinian lover, Beirut has now become the (unattainable) beloved. Nowhere is this seen with more startling force than in Darwish's *Ode*, which reads as part-paean and part-love song to his adopted (or adoptive) home. Here, he extols the city's beauty with his cry: »An apple for the sea, a marble narcissus / A butterfly of stone: Beirut« (89), underscoring the totality of his identification with her with the descriptor »shape of the soul reflected« (89) and the lines: »Beirut is a witness to my heart / I depart from her streets and from myself« (94). Similarly, he pronounces in *Eulogy*: »Beirut is our image / Beirut is our *sura*« (28), a *sura* being a *Qur'anic* verse. Claiming Beirut as his »sweetheart« (*habiba*), Darwish explains in *Ode* how, for the diminished and enfeebled Palestinians, she has become »our only tent« and »our only star« (91), while in *Eulogy* he rues that she is »our citadel [...] our tear« (8) and »our story, [...] our torment« (11). Further, to this rootless population, she offers a vantage point on their homeland, the Arab nations and the world beyond.

For Darwish, a wondrous, if problematic, characteristic of Beirut is that she permits all those who dwell in her to recreate her in their own image. He describes Beirut as »the song of everyone without a homeland« (Darwish 1995, 60), exile in his vernacular pertaining to more than a mere fact of geographical situation. Beirut is at once an anthem and a haven for the region's dispossessed, cast out and oppressed, though this offers a representation that is more strictly pan-Arab than cosmopolitan *per se*. As he

14 One literary associate identified in *Memory* is the Pakistani poet Faiz Ahmad Faiz (1914–1984), who edited *Lotus* magazine from exile in Beirut.

explains in *Memory* (92), Beirut's porosity and plasticity present the paradox of a city where the sum of its parts appears to be greater than the whole:

»For the political refugee, there's a chair that can't be changed or replaced [...] For the refugee merchant there's the opportunity to discover that the winds of the '50s, which promised something to the Arab poor, will not blow this way again. For the writer whose country is too confining, [...] there's the freedom to believe he's free, without knowing on which front he's fighting. For the ex-poet, there's the possibility of getting hold of a pistol, a guard and money [...] assassinating a critic here and bribing another there. For the traditional young woman, there's the chance to make her veil disappear into her handbag on the steps of an aeroplane, then to disappear into a hotel room with her lover. [...]Every visitor to Beirut finds his own special city, and we don't know – no-one does – to what extent all these cities make up the city of Beirut.«

Thus, the terrible appeal of Beirut is her inauthenticity, and her willingness to be all things to all who inhabit her. Besides being foster mother and sweetheart, in *Ode* (105) she is also the signifiers »sea«, »war«, »ink« and »profit« (*bahr – harb – hibr – ribh*), a mercenary whore, and a sunflower turning her head to the sun. She is a city that creates just as much as she devastates: »Beirut is the form of form / The architect of destruction« (110). Though it is Beirut's very inauthenticity that permits Darwish to write and even exist, his ambivalence towards her multiplicity is clear.

Memory in particular describes how the problematic of Beirut's cosmopolitics was hardened definitively by the realities of war. It is understood that a cosmopolitan milieu is one »in which the various groups are not forced to choose between ghettoization and assimilation« (Yerasimos 1999, 36). In Beirut, the war definitively reversed the cosmopolitan phenomenon: urban space became redistributed and divided according to sectarian alignment (as with »Muslim« West Beirut and the »Christian« East), and this plural society became subject to new closures and boundaries, with communal and religious authority resurrected at its heart. In the wake of the Sabra and Shatila refugee camp massacres, Darwish (1985, 138) laments: »Sectarian wolves have taken over the nation [...] the Palestinian problem is the scandal of the nation«. Ironically, and tragically, it was in part the pluralistic, cosmopolitan milieu of Beirut's »golden age« that had expedited and enabled the Lebanese conflict, Darwish explaining in *Memory* (134–5):

»Beirut [...] became the property of anyone who dreamed of a different political order elsewhere and accommodated the chaos that for every exile resolved the complex of being an exile. [...] The refugee in the city no longer felt the need to worry about the collapsing order; rather, by allowing himself freely to form alliances within it, [...] he helped only to speed up that collapse.«

Though Darwish foregrounds his allegiance to Beirut's beleaguered Palestinians, within the broader context of Israel's siege, he appears to intimate that they owe their hosting community special service. In *Memory* (162), we see the »Palestinian Poet Laureate« place his poetry to one side, and declare: »There is no role for me in poetry now. My role is outside the poem. My role is to be here, with the citizens and the fighters.« Thus, Palestinians do battle alongside Lebanese in defending the city of Beirut from its aggressor, for the sake of justice and the common good – and in defence of their »very existence« (40). Lauding the Palestinians' heroic shielding of the Lebanese capital, Darwish proclaims: »Let Beirut be what she wants to be / This, our blood raised high for her / Is an unbending tree« (152–3). In equal measure, he pillories the international community and, above all, the Arab regimes for their callous abandonment of both Palestinians and Lebanese to Israel's onslaught.

As Darwish's Beirut texts confirm, the city during the war was no longer cosmopolitan, but a shattered *polis* formed from »brutal exchanges of population and ethnic cleansing, together with the influx of refugees from the mountains or from South Lebanon« (Davie 2008, 319). With the Sabra and Shatila massacres, Darwish was compelled to confront the horrors of Lebanese Phalangists exterminating Palestinians with Israeli backing. Displaying a mordant pride that transmutes rapidly to dismay, he observes that the Palestinians in Lebanon

»[...] taught their murderers the value of fighting for liberty; they were the ones who transported them through camaraderie and fine example from tears of complaint and deprivation to fight in defence of justice and homeland; they were the ones who sowed the traditions of steadfastness and heroism in south Lebanon. They were the same ones who established a new climate for resisting the occupation, who gave their lives resisting the invasion side by side with those who are killing them now. They are the ones who, dare I say, helped create their murderers of today« (Darwish 1985, 140).

Throughout these texts, Darwish's devotion to Beirut, his foster mother, remains unabated, to the extent that he accepts that a Palestinian victory in Lebanon would have been hateful, if not morally unconscionable. Indeed, his gratitude to the city is both humble and unremitting, as when he celebrates his surviving one more day of that terrible siege, crying in *Ode* (95):

»Thank you to Beirut in the mist! / Thank you to Beirut in ruins!« Such is his cherishing of his city-sweetheart that he affirms that he transports her wherever his destiny takes him: »I fold the city like I fold a book«, he says, »And carry that little bit of land like a sack of clouds« (94). Extending a heartfelt farewell to the city that, for nine years, has homed him, he acknowledges that he must leave for the sake of her future survival, conceding finally in *Eulogy* (90): »My homeland *is* a suitcase«.

Conclusion

In today's Middle East, it would not be unreasonable to suggest that cosmopolitanism has become »a rare phenomenon, something of the past, when borders had not yet been clearly demarcated and identities had not yet been defined or jealously defended« (Meijer 1999, 2). With the Israeli invasion, and eventual occupation, of Beirut – the first Arab capital after Palestine to succumb to such a fate – its »crucial role in the making of modern Arab culture also ended. By the time the people of Beirut bid their thundering farewell to the Palestinian forces, most members of the Arab intelligentsia who had made their home in Beirut had long gone, and the Palestinian artists who remained were soon dispersed« (Boullata 2003, 24). Further, this once multicultural and multiconfessional society had become riven by xenophobic, sectarian and class-based hostilities. Thus it may be argued that, today, Beirut's »cosmopolitanism« is chiefly symbolic, a vestige of a glamorised, romanticised national past, a nostalgic myth, an ideal, a fanciful synonym for »globalisation«.

And what of Darwish, the »citizen of the world«? In the face of deracination and the possibility of cultural erasure, Darwish – like so many other Palestinians – maintained his own forms of particularism, be this in Israel, Lebanon or other outposts of the Palestinian diaspora. Just as significantly, his combined output demonstrates how, with his multiple locations of »home«, he continued to finesse and individualise his identity, while eluding the fanaticism of patriots and the homogenisation of internationalists. An eclectic writer who sought to dialogue with many cultures, Darwish was at once an identifiably Palestinian poet, while being simultaneously claimed for Arab and world poetry. His championing of the Palestinian cause was founded on humanist, rather than nationalist, principles, indeed, he came to problematise, if not vilify, vulgar nationalist rhetoric, as we may see in his challenge to the ousted Palestinian fighter in *Eulogy* (119): »What is it you want? / As you march from legend to legend / A flag? / What good have flags ever done? / *Have they ever protected a city from the shrapnel of a bomb?*«

Works cited

Boullata, Kamal (Summer 2003). Artists Remember Palestine in Beirut. *Journal of Palestine Studies*, 32:4, 22–38.

Darwish, Mahmud (1984). Qasidat Bayrut. In *Hisar li-Mada'ih al-Bahr*, 87–116. Beirut: Dar al-'Awda.

Darwish, Mahmud (1993). *Madih al-Zill al-'Ali*. Beirut: Dar al-'Awda.

Darwish, Mahmud (1985). The Madness of Being a Palestinian. *Journal of Palestine Studies*, 15:1, 138–41.

Darwish, Mahmud (1995). *Memory for Forgetfulness: August, Beirut, 1982*, trans. I. Muhawi. Berkeley: University of California Press.

Darwish, Mahmud (1998). »There is No Meaning to My Life Outside Poetry«. *BANIPAL. Magazine of Modern Arab Literature* 4, http://www.banipal.co.uk/selections/selection.php?workid=157 (accessed 27 March 2009).

Darwish, Mahmud (2002). A Love Story Between an Arab Poet and His Land. *Journal of Palestine Studies*, 31:3, 67–78.

Davie, Michael F. (2008). Imagining Beirut's Reconstructed City Centre. In Robin Ostle (ed.). *Sensibilities of the Islamic Mediterranean*, 313–29. London: I.B. Tauris.

Khalaf, Samir (2002). *Civil and Uncivil Violence in Lebanon: A History of the Internationalization of Communal Conflict*. New York: Columbia University Press.

Meijer, Roel (1999). Introduction. In Roel Meijer (ed.). *Cosmopolitanism, Identity and Authenticity in the Middle East*, 2–13. Richmond, Surrey: Curzon.

Sa'di, Ahmad H. (2002). Catastrophe, Memory and Identity: *Al-Nakbah* as a Component of Palestinian Identity. *Israel Studies*, 7:2, 175–98.

Yerasimos, Stéphane (1999). Cosmopolitanism: Assumed Alienation. In Roel Meijer (ed.). *Cosmopolitanism, Identity and Authenticity in the Middle East*, 35–9. Richmond, Surrey: Curzon.

Zubeida, Sami (1999). Cosmopolitanism and the Middle East. In Roel Meijer (ed.). *Cosmopolitanism, Identity and Authenticity in the Middle East*, 15–33. Richmond, Surrey: Curzon.

Contributors

Liam Chambers is a lecturer in the Department of History at Mary Immaculate College, University of Limerick. His publications include *Rebellion in Kildare, 1790–1803* (Dublin: Four Courts Press, 1998) and *Michael Moore, c.1639–1726: Provost of Trinity, Rector of Paris* (Dublin: Four Courts Press, 2005). He is currently working on the history of theIrish Colleges in Paris, 1578–2000, for which he was awarded an IRCHSS (Irish Research Council for the Humanities and Social Sciences) Government of Ireland Research Fellowship in 2005–2006.

Kate Daniels is a lecturer in Modern Arabic Language, Literature and Arab Film at the Faculty of Asian and Middle Eastern Studies, University of Cambridge. She is Director of Studies in Asian and Middle Eastern Studies at Newnham College, Cambridge. Her publications include *Literary and Historical Interpretations and Representations of Early Arab Christian Migration to the Americas'*, in: Religious Refugees in Europe, Asia and the Americas, 6th-21st Centuries, ed. Susanne Lachenicht, p. 247–274 (Hamburg u.a.: LIT-Verlag 2007) and *Self and Other: The Short Fiction of Yusuf al-Sharuni* (Piscataway, NJ: Gorgias Press 2009).

Frank Grüner leads the interdisciplinary Junior Research Group »Asia and Europe in a Global Context« (University of Heidelberg) on »Transgressing Spaces and Identities in Urban Arenas – the Case of Harbin«. From 2003 to 2005 he was a lecturer and from 2005 to 2008 Assistant Professor in East European History at the University of Heidelberg. His publications include: *Patrioten und Kosmopoliten. Juden im Sowjetstaat 1941 bis 1953.* (Cologne u.a.: Böhlau 2008) and (as editor) *»Zerstörer des Schweigens«. Formen künstlerischer Erinnerung an die nationalsozialistische Rassen- und Vernichtungspolitik in Osteuropa.* (Cologne u.a.: Böhlau 2006) (with U. Heftrich and H.-D. Löwe).

Kirsten Heinsohn is a research fellow at the Institute for German-Jewish History in Hamburg and a lecturer of the Department of History at Hamburg University, Germany. She has published books and articles on German Conservatives and Gender History and she is now working on the biography of Eva Reichmann (1897–1998) Her publications include: (as editor): *Deutsch-Jüdische Geschichte als Geschlechtergeschichte. Eine Zwischenbilanz.* (Göttingen: Wallstein, 2006) (with Stefanie Schüler-Springorum). Germany, in: Kevin Passmore (ed.). *Women, Gender and Fascism in Europe 1919–1945.* (Manchester: Manchester University Press 2003), p. 33–56.

Anna Holian is Assistant Professor of History at Arizona State University. She is the author of *Between National Socialism and Soviet Communism: Displaced Persons in Postwar Germany* (University of Michigan Press, forthcoming). Her current research focuses on representations of »war children« in postwar European film and on spatial practices and conflicts over space in early postwar Germany.

Maurizio Isabella is a lecturer in Modern European History at Queen Mary College, London University. He has held fellowships at Birkbeck Colege, London, and Princeton University. He has written several articles and chapters in edited volumes on the *Risorgimento*, focussing in particular on exile and on economic and political thought. He is the author of *Risorgimento in Exile. Italian émigrés and the Liberal International in the Post-Napoleonic Era* (Oxford: Oxford University Press 2009).

Susanne Lachenicht is a lecturer in Early Modern History at Hamburg University. She is the author of *Information und Propaganda. Die Presse deutscher Jakobiner im Elsaß (1791–1800)* (Munich: Oldenbourg 2004) and *Hugenotten in Europa und Nordamerika. Immigrationspolitik und Integrationsprozesse in der Frühen Neuzeit (1548–1787)* (forthcoming Frankfurt/Main–New York: Campus 2010). She is editor of *Religious Refugees in Europe, Asia and North America (6th–21st century)* (Hamburg: LIT–Verlag 2007) and (with G. Braun) *Les États allemands et les huguenots. Politique d'immigration et processus d'intégration* (Munich : Oldenbourg 2007).

Bertrand Van Ruymbeke is professor of American history at the Université de Paris VIII at Saint-Denis. He is the author of *From New Babylon to Eden. The Huguenot and Their Migration to Colonial South Carolina*, (Columbia: University of South Carolina Press 2006) and co-editor (with R. Sparks) of *Memory and Idendity. The Huguenots in France and the Atlantic Diaspora* (Columbia: University of South Carolina Press 2003), *Constructing Early Modern Empires. Proprietary Ventures in the Atlantic World, 1550–1700* (Leiden : Brill 2007).